Free Gifts

Dear Reader

I want to thank you for buying this book. Whether you did it out of sheer curiosity regarding what the book is about, or you did out of your faith and trust in me due to our existing relationship, I am glad that you now have one of the most honest personal finance document in your hands.

Before we get started, I'd like to invite you to head over to the resources mentioned at the bottom of this letter. These are free gifts you get from my company for being a valued reader. The purpose of these gifts is to expand upon what I have said in the book, or to compliment the ideas in the book.

You are welcome to sign up for free, download them all right away, and consume those resources as and when you are ready. The best way to do it would be to sign up for the resources right now, and start reading the book. As you read, you will see me call out the need for you to access a particular resource. That would be the ideal time for you to access the respective free gift.

Wishing You Lifelong Prosperity

P.S. If you would like my team to use all the principles detailed in this book and manage your wealth, I welcome you to visit www.BehlCap.com and explore the various opportunities currently available.

- Master List of Gifts: www.lakshaybehl.com/wealth-gifts
- Financial Calculators: www.LakshayBehl.com/Calculators
- Lakshay Behl's Official Newsletter (Complimentary 1 month subscription with code "201456wealth"): www.LakshayBehl.com/NewsLetter

4

LAKSHAY BEHL is the world's leading business systems architect. He is in the business of creating systems for companies that he co-owns, or that his clients own. He works with small and medium enterprises to automate sales and marketing systems, and to automate production and fulfillment systems... so that the teams can stop worrying about day-to-day running of the business, and focus on the things that require true creativity. Like innovating and coming up with offers that add value to their customers' lives.

Lakshay was born in 1989, and started exhibiting signs of entrepreneurial tendencies as early as 1994... when he bought firecrackers during the daytimes, and sell them to other kids on his street during the nighttime when they would run out of their own stock, and shops would be closed for the day. Over his childhood and early adolescence, he engaged in many other similar capitalistic ventures that relied on customers' needs and demands. He was brought up in poverty, and his mother was the only earning member of a family of four. On a meager salary of two hundred Dollars a month, she enrolled both her sons in a school that would normally be inaccessible to someone with her financial capacity. She devoted as much as forty percent of her income towards just the education of her sons. That often left her with very little money to cover rent, bills, and groceries. Lakshay's pocket money came from his own capitalistic endeavors that at times greatly aggravated his superiors who considered him insolent.

His first big break came when he was only 13 years old. In the year 2002, Lakshay was forced to negotiate a real estate on behalf of his parents. Due to unavoidable legal circumstances, his parents, the rightful owners were not present for the deal, even though losing the deal would mean they would have to incur deep financial losses that wouldn't be easy to recover from. So they placed a great deal of trust in Lakshay and appointed him to negotiate on their behalf. While everyone including the brokers and the potential buyer underestimated Lakshay, he played them all by acting aloof and indifferent where his parents would have been very accommodating... and consequently ended up getting 37% more than the minimum his parents would have accepted.

The broker involved in the deal was so impressed with Lakshay that he offered him a weekends-only part time job, where he would be charged with helping with the negotiations. The salary offered was $50 a month. Shortly afterwards, Lakshay was offered another freelancing job at a nightclub where he was charged with bringing in new guests. By the time Lakshay was sixteen, he was already earning as much as his mother, and contributed to the family income.

At the age of sixteen, after cracking the Joint Entrance Examination in his first attempt, an exam universally regarded as one of the hardest exams to crack, Lakshay started teaching Physics and Mathematics to students, who were often older than him. A few months into the teaching job, he was very publicly reprimanded rather brutally for a perceived slight he had incurred towards his employers. On that day, Lakshay pledged never to work for anyone else ever again.

1

That event was followed by a string of business failures. Lakshay started twelve businesses over the course of next three years, and all of them failed. Yet, they thought him valuable lessons about life and business, about trust and friendship, and about treachery and scams that would guide him forever.

Those valuable business and life lessons have since propelled him to create and grow many successful businesses over the years. Today, Lakshay is primarily charged with growing his clients' businesses. Clients often relinquish most of their responsibilities as well as power for a set period of time to Lakshay, and Lakshay dictates all the necessary changes to be made. As a consequence, businesses end up completely systemized, so that the teams are free to focus on growing the companies, instead of running them.

Lakshay has been involved behind the closed doors with many companies, and at the time of writing this book, has been responsible for as many as eighteen "six figures in 24 hours" product launches, and four "seven figures in 24 hours" launches. He has worked with companies in the United States, in Europe, Australia, India, Japan and Thailand, in many different industries including, but not limited to Hospitality, Digital, Technology, Finance, Real Estate, Gaming, Music, Event Management, Manufacturing, Education and Politics.

Wired To Be Poor is Lakshay's first book. It is governed by the guiding philosophy of his life that "the world works the way it does, not the way you want it to". The book contains rules that govern the creation and accumulation of wealth, and comes as a guidebook containing the set of rules one needs to win at the game of wealth accumulation.

The book starts with an examination of the nature of money, its neutrality, and the emotional associations that often keep people from accepting the true nature of money. Then it follows the course of human history to examine why money appears to be mysterious to the human mind. Thereafter, the book examines the various ways of accumulating wealth. Finally, the book concludes with a brief summary of maxims that represent the rules for winning the game, and that make success inevitable.

Wired

To Be Poor

**Why Most People Will Never Accumulate
Significant Wealth In Their Lifetime**

LAKSHAY BEHL

INNOVATE **LEVERAGING** MAXIMIZE
250 YEARS

Behl Capital

MANAGED INVESTMENTS

MERGERS & ACQUISITIONS

Dear Sarthak

While you are my brother, I have always treated you like my son.

I dedicate this book to you in hope that you will keep these lessons in mind while making all major financial decisions in your life.

Lakshay

Table of Contents

WEALTH IS EVIL?

Let us examine the nature of wealth.

Money and wealth is rarely, if ever, free of connotations. And emotional association.

Whether this emotional association is positive or negative, it is rather profound for almost everyone old enough to understand the concept of money. Whether the connotations associated with money are positive or negative, the connotations are there, and they are invariably significant.

What this means is this...

People can either like money, and the concept of it... Or dislike it. But it is rare for someone to be emotionally unaffected by it.

People can either have enough money, or not. But rarely do you meet someone who is completely devoid of emotionality about the subject.

And before we dive into what money is, what wealth is, how they are different, and most importantly… why most people on the face of this planet are wired to be poor… I want to spend a few minutes talking about, and hopefully dissociating, money and its emotional content.

How many times have you heard the following phrase…

"Love Of Money Is The Root Of All Evil"

I am sure, many times.

Do you agree with it? Or do you disagree?

Chances are, that since you are about to read a book related to personal finance, you are more likely to disagree with it. Even though the world around us is filled with numerous examples and case studies that validate that statement.

I mean… look around.

Look at any news channel or news paper. Every single day, almost every story that is unrelated to personal vengeance or international politics is related to money. Somebody scamming someone. Someone murdering someone else to steal. Someone lying and cheating for monetary gain.

Yet, at the same time you read about Bill Gates donating tens of Millions of Dollars for one charitable cause after another. He's got more money than he can ever hope to spend. And he undoubtedly is using it for many worthy causes.

And he's not alone.

There are many famous and wealthy people who donate regularly for worthy causes. In fact, it's not just wealthy celebrities who donate. You yourself, quite possibly, donate for some causes. And you are undoubtedly acquainted with, or related to many other people who do the same.

Quite naturally, one's ability and propensity to donate is directly proportional to their income... For if one is barely earning enough to make the ends meet... it is unlikely that he'll donate for a cause, no matter how worthy.

Having said that, I'll now get to the point.

Money is neither evil nor a force of good.

Money is just a tool.

That's right.

Just a tool. Like a hammer, or a nail. Or a saw.

You can use a saw to chop of someone's fingers... or you can use it to cut wood and construct a house for someone to live in.

You can use a hammer to break into someone's private safe and steal money… or you can use it to hammer nails into wood build furniture.

Money is entirely neutral.

It can be used for good. It can be used for evil. And it can be used to acquire more wealth.

The sooner you understand this, the sooner you get over the mental hurdles that will keep most people mired in poverty.

Now, just to be clear… Money is NOT wealth. And I spend a good portion of the next few sections explaining that point. Wealth is good by virtue of being, and it will become clear to you as you read ahead.

But as far as money is concerned…as far as the coins and bills in your pocket and wallet are concerned… it's just neutral. There is nothing inherently bad about it. Just as there is nothing inherently admirable about money.

Do You Admire Or Disdain People With A Lot Of Money?

It helps to think of money as toothpaste.

Would you admire someone simply because they had a lot more toothpaste on their shelf than you do?

And in the same vein… would you be envious of someone who had a lot more toothpaste than you? And would you treat them with disdain or contempt?

Of course not!

Yet, when it comes to money… there is a real possibility that you might respect someone just because they have a lot more money in their bank account than you do. Or disdain them. Or be envious of them.

If you automatically accord respect or admiration to someone simply because they have money… or any other emotion for that matter, then you have an emotional relationship with money.

This emotional relationship is like a barrier.

A barrier that prevents you from accepting the true nature of money. The nature that we will discuss in great detail over the course of this book.

Now, there is a very real reason why this barrier exists. It's not abnormal, heavens no. And it's certainly not uncommon.

The reason why it exists, and is so prominent as well as widespread is because there seems to be a causal relationship between money and effort.

Most children are brought up watching their parents expend a great deal of effort in order to make money. They see their parents work two jobs in order to make more money. They see their elders sacrifice their health, their freedom, and even their relationships just so they can make more money.

Naturally, they conclude that the way to make more money is working harder, and longer hours.

Naturally, there is a connection in their minds between number of hours spent working each day, and quality of lifestyle afforded by the money earned.

Then, we are all bombarded with news about people stealing from each other, murdering each other and scamming each other just to make more money… and one might instinctively conclude that there is no way to make enormous sums of money… Unless you do something unethical, or somehow get lucky.

Naturally, most people think that the only way they can get rich is by winning the lottery. Which, let's face it… doesn't happen. Can not happen. The numbers are just not in your favor.

In fact, if you have find yourself buying a lottery ticket, stop. It's actually better if you just put those ten Dollars in a bank account… boring as it might be.

To be sure, putting money in a bank account won't ever make you rich. But it's better than buying a lottery ticket.

Obvious, right?

Well, if it were so obvious… companies selling lottery tickets would have been out of business. Yet, as it happens… these companies have flourished over the centuries. Millions of people buy lottery tickets regularly. Most of them do it secretly.

But they do it nevertheless. But I digress.

The point is… people think money is hard to get. People think that money works in mysterious ways. And that the only sure shot way to make more money is to work harder, and to work longer hours. Or to go to college and then work harder.

Fortunately, none of that is true.

Fortunately, money does not work in mysterious ways. While there is no proven formula, accumulation of wealth always boils down to a few fundamental principles. Principles that remain largely unaffected by the era that we live in.

And should you observe carefully, you will see strict adherence to these principles behind every success story that you hear.

In the upcoming sections, I will ensure that these principles are made clear to you. So that you may go out, and observe for yourself how every fortune ever accumulated is on account of an almost dogmatic adherence to them.

And finally, so that you yourself may start playing the game well.

Speaking of games... there are two sets of rules for every game. The first set of rules has to do with the playing of the game. And the second set has to do with winning.

When Warren Buffet decided to learn to play the game of Bridge, he hired a former champion to teach him the rules. He said, and I might be paraphrasing here... "I want to learn the rules of winning at Bridge, not just playing it."

This book contains a set of rules and principles.

This set is similar not to the "How to Play" set, but to the "How to Win" set.

Lastly, I want to make it very clear that this is not a "Get Rich Quick" method. In fact, I don't think those exist at all. The only fast way of becoming wealthy is starting a business that grows extremely rapidly.

And while there is a scientific method of growing a business with extreme rapidity... I am actually in the business of doing just that... I must confess that it has far more to do with the environment than the actions of the business leader himself.

I will discuss some of the tenets of rapid wealth production in one of the sections in the book.

At the same time, I should make it very clear... that accumulation of wealth takes time. A long time. It doesn't happen overnight. Every overnight success story is preceded by many, MANY years of hard work, experimentation and learning. Years spent in darkness and obscurity.

Now, you don't have to spend years in obscurity. You don't even need to become an overnight success. If you just follow the principles laid out in the following pages, you'll accumulate your own fortune slowly, yet steadily.

With that said, let's dive into the meat of this book, and let us examine a very unfortunate fact about our relationship with wealth.

WE ARE WIRED TO BE POOR

Let's begin with the bad news. We are all wired to be poor. Biologically and instinctively, our cybernetic* system is wired to be poor. Not only poor, but we are all wired to be fat, lazy and selfish.

And in the next few minutes, I am going to show you why.

So that's the bad news. But I also have some very good news. The good news is actually inherent in that bad news. Like a cocoon hides and protects the tiny little life inside, the bad news (that we are all wired to be poor) hides good news on the inside. But before I tell you what this good news is, let me dwell on the bad news for a few minutes.

So...

We are all wired to be poor. And broke. To explain this phenomenon, I'll make use of a field of study called evolutionary psychology.

10

Wealth from an Evolutionary Perspective

Most people believe that human beings evolved from lower and less intelligent life forms, namely apes. And that we are genetically closest to two species of apes: The Bonobos and the Gorillas. That is the basic theory of evolution.

This process of evolution is not instantaneous. It does not happen over the course of years. Evolution does not take place over the course of lifetimes. In fact, even over a few dozen generations, the effects of evolution are barely visible.

Evolution takes millions of years.

Now, whether or not you believe in the theory of evolution is irrelevant to this discussion from a financial standpoint. You don't have to believe in it if it goes against your religious beliefs. Or for that matter, any other beliefs of yours. But for now, the implications of this theory are too logical and practical for us to ignore. As an intelligent investor, I urge you to keep an open mind, and observe at least one possible reason why most people do what they do, and why most people are going to stay poor for the rest of their lives.

Ready?

For millions of years, as apes evolved into human beings – there was no money. In fact, the conception of money is fairly new. Money was invented just a few thousand years ago.

For the longest periods of time, human beings (or whatever they were back then without agriculture, tools, laws and language) lived in small tribes. Most of these tribes had 30 -70 members. That number includes men, women and children.

The job of the men was to go out and to hunt animals. That's what men did all day long. Especially when the weather was good, that's what they did.

Another part of their job was to protect their land (on which the tribe resided), their women and their possessions from bands of other men.

Good stretches of land were often won through paying by blood. Pieces of land close to rivers, that had lots of animals who strolled by, and had trees laden with fruit were attractive to all men.

People from tribes that lived on relatively barren lands strived to move to better lands, which were invariably preoccupied by another tribe. For this reason, men from tribes went out and fought local wars. To gain control of lands, and other resources that were precious and valuable.

And what was valuable?

Well, imagine you are a tribal man. Or a caveman. You live with your woman and children in a small tribe. You don't know much about communication, and you don't know much about arts, or math, or science, or philosophy, or even language. The way you eat is by hunting. That is also how you provide for your woman (or women) and children.

The job of women in those days was to go out and gather fruit from trees. Mostly fruit that had already fallen. Along with the low hanging fruit. That's what women did.

Now… if this primitive life was yours, **what would you consider to be valuable?**

The answer is simple… Whatever helps you hunt more food. Be it land close to water so that thirsty animals would naturally be drawn to it… or land fertile enough to grow trees laden with fruits, it was valuable.

Indeed, food must have been the most valuable resource for survival back in those days.

And anything that helped you feed yourself and your family was worth fighting for.

If a piece of land could feed cattle, that you could raise and kill for meat and other products, that would become valuable, right?

And this is how the concept of real estate was born.

Today, we don't fight for land. We simply buy it in exchange for money, or something else of definitive dollar value.

But if there were no laws, and no money to exchange, and the only reason someone had a piece of land was because they were sitting on it – and the only reason why you didn't have it because you weren't sitting on it, wouldn't you fight for it?

Of course you would.

And that is what our ancestors did.

So you see, they lived in a world of scarcity. We'll talk more about scarcity and abundance in Section 2. (Wealth Creation Principles)

Back in the day, any man with a lucrative, fertile stretch of land, with trees and plants laden with fruits and vegetables on it, and hoards of cattle to chew on the grass and provide milk, meat and hide… as well as the physical might to protect it from intruders, trespassers and interlopers would be a rich man.

Such a man (and his tribe) had very good chances to survive. Not only would they have the most resources for survival, but also for replication. The best women would often live in such tribes. And the children would also have the chance to survive, grow safely, become strong and then go on to reproduce in such an environment.

OK…

So **what else had value back then?**

Well, tools did. Why? Let's take a very simple example.

Say men of a tribe went to war with men of another tribe. Now, which tribe had a better chance at winning this war? Of course, it would depend upon the physical strength, the courage and the sheer number of men on either side. But it also depended upon the kind of warfare technology and tools they had.

So clearly, ways to create stronger walls in order to keep out intruders became important.

By the way, the consequences of losing such a war were too severe. See, if your tribe lost, not only would you be executed, but your male offsprings too would be killed in cold blood. The reasons were many, but this is what happened most commonly. The women would be raped, and ultimately, the best looking women would be betrothed to the strongest conquering men based on the social hierarchy.

So tools, and their inventors started having a lot of value and significance.

As evolution continued, human beings discovered agriculture. And fire and cooking. The value of fertile land that could be used for agriculture skyrocketed. Most wars back in those days were wars of greed.

Actually, most wars that human beings wage on each other even today are wars of greed. A significant reason why one country attacks another is because of its resources. Natural and man made. Often, today's wars are waged under the veneer of "doing the right thing" and "establishing a proper democratic government" but this veneer is often quite thin and rather transparent if you think about it carefully enough.

As evolution processed, and as human beings progressed, the tribes started getting bigger. Since the discovery of agriculture, food became rather abundant. Human beings didn't need to depend purely on hunting and gathering for survival anymore. They could grow their crops and feed everyone.

When the food was scarce, tribes would often sacrifice their "dead weight". For instance, a man who suffered an ailment, and could not pull his own weight was ruthlessly culled and left out to fend for himself... which often meant he'd not survive longer than a couple of weeks.

But once food became abundant, tribes didn't stay as lean as they used to stay previously.

Then, with the invention of civil engineering technology, masonry, and the building of stronger walls... as well as better tools to not only hunt animals with, but also to fight off any outsiders with became available, a lesser number of men were needed for protecting the entire tribe. While earlier, almost every man who couldn't fight was culled, and almost every man in the tribe was a warrior primarily, now only a small minority of men would engage in hunting and defense.

Tribes became societies and men who were not warriors started doing other things. Some became farmers, and traded produce from their farms with other people for other things of value. This system was known as bartering. This was the basic form of economics as it evolved.

As the human societies progressed, the percentage of men who were full time warriors continued reducing. What percent of men enlist in the military today? The answer is, that for most western nations, this number is less than 1%.

So as societies evolved, and as technology evolved, less and less men were needed to protect the boundary walls. But, as technology evolved, even on the farm inside, fewer men could do what a larger number of men could previously do. And as a consequence, many men were no longer required to farm either.

So they started choosing other professions. Like story telling, or arts, or mathematics, or philosophy. And a breed of softer men was born.

In the hierarchy, these men were not ranked on the basis of their physical strength or courage in the battlefield, but on the basis of their proficiency in whatever they did.

An artist would be judged on the basis of the emotional content of his art. A story teller would be judged on the basis of how much attention his stories could garner. So on and so forth.

The Invention of Money

In the meanwhile, the need for a monetary system became evident.

Say you have a herd of 100 cattle. And you don't need that many this year. In fact, you won't be needing more than 20 cattle for the next three years.

But you would like to have mangoes that have been ripening in my little garden.

So you would like to barter some of your cattle for my mangoes, right?

And the trade should be easy enough.

Except, I don't want any cattle. I have no need for cattle. I only consume milk, and I get more than enough from my brother, who also happens to be a herder of cattle.

This made commerce very difficult.

And so money was invented.

Now, keep in mind, the invention of money is relatively recent. On an evolutionary time scale, that lasts across hundreds of thousands of years, the invention of money is fairly recent.

Around 5000 BC (that's 7000 years ago) human beings started trading pieces of metal. Those pieces of metal became currency back then.

Understanding Money & Currencies

Let us first address what money and currency really truly mean.

The value of a piece of metal is zero. It is, it was, and it almost always will be.

Unless you can use that piece of metal to do something with it, like reform it into a piece of jewelry, or a hammer to nail your enemies coffins with, the value of that piece of metal is zero.

And yet, metal was used as a currency.

Why?

Because it is readily available, easy to work with, and easy to recycle.

Now you take a piece of metal, and attach a symbolic value to it. It then becomes money.

Money is, and has never been, anything more than a symbol for wealth. Money is simply a tool that lubricates commerce.

That's it.

So instead of carrying around a ton of cattle to trade, you could sell those cattle for money. And then use that money to buy mangoes from me, and meat from a hunter, and an abacus from a mathematician. And then use some money to buy jewelry for your woman who happens to be overtly fond of things like flowers and jewelry and face paints.

(Please note: I have deliberately downplayed the role of women in this Section on Evolutionary theory. That does not mean women had no impact on the course of our evolution. Of course women drove the process of evolution just as much as men did, if not more. I just didn't emphasize what they did because it is irrelevant to our understanding of finance.)

This conception of money made life far too simple for everyone.

Soon, our ancestors figured out that all things are not created equal, and therefore, must be priced differently.

Things that were scarce, such as fertile land, became available for sale only for large amounts of money. Things that were abundant, such as wheat and corn, became available for small amounts of money.

And so economic indices were formed.

Today, our economic indices have become far more sophisticated. Prices are driven by demand and supply. Demand and supply are driven by, and modified by technological, political, social and economic factors far beyond the control, or even understanding of the most aware economists.

But the basic principle still applies... Easily obtainable commodities are still cheap. Prized articles are steeply priced.

OK. So what has all this got to do with you?

Answer: A lot!

This basically explains why you, and I, and every other human being on the face of this planet is wired to be poor.

But before I explain that, let's take a minute to visit the fundamental premise of the evolutionary theory.

The Evolutionary Theory states that...

Most of our instincts and emotions are those of the caveman, and the early tribesman that our distant ancestors were.

Human species have progressed at an unprecedented rate. Our cybernetic systems have not yet had a chance to evolve. Cybernetic systems take many, many generations to evolve.

As a consequence, most of how we feel and consequently, what we do, is dictated by how our caveman ancestors would have felt and what they would have done.

Now, money is a recent invention in terms of evolutionary timescales. And therefore, our minds are not wired to handle money correctly. Allow me to explain.

Wired To Spend Immediately

Remember the example where you had an abundance of cattle that you wanted to trade in for my mangoes and the hunter's meat?

Well, if you didn't make the trade fast enough, you could actually lose your cattle to sickness, disease, malnutrition, weather, or other harsh factors in the environment.

And as a mango seller, if I didn't get rid of my mangoes fast enough by either bartering them with something of value, or by eating them all, they would rot and become valueless.

Clearly, things that we held dear for most of our evolutionary history were perishable resources.

And since these resources were perishable, we wanted to spend them immediately. And that was quite natural, right?

Unfortunately, spending our valuables became our instinct.

Today, we understand that money is valuable. Yet spending it gives us a sort of a buzz or a high. The same dopamine release that you would have gotten by either consuming meat, or by bartering meat for something else of value, if you lived in a primitive society.

Since our cybernetic system doesn't instinctively understand that money is not perishable, storing money is inevitably quite the challenge for us. We naturally enjoy spending, and we want to spend.

Now there is one important exception to this rule. There happens to be one particular thing that we are hard wired to never let go of. Can you think what it might be?

It's real estate.

Human beings have been fighting for ownership and control over pieces of land for a long, long time. Even from an evolutionary perspective, the desire to own land is hard wired into human psyche.

This is why you see people getting very emotional about buying and selling real estate. Especially if someone is forced to sell owing to a lack of financial ability, they tend to become very emotionally sad and anxious.

But other than real estate, we don't have any cybernetic conception of money. We don't realize it's nothing more than a tool to acquire whatever it is that we need to acquire.

Hence, we are wired to spend much of what we earn quite quickly. This is why you see people running out of cash towards the end of the month.

As the payday approaches, they plan their shopping

activities. Then as soon as they get paid, they spend a good deal of their income on products and services that they need... and also on products and services that they want.

But most importantly, they also spend money on buying things that they neither need, nor even truly want, but just feel like getting. Worse, they end up buying things that promised to themselves they would not buy. Like a pack of fattening and health destroying highly processed foods that don't even taste delicious if you chew slowly.

Sometimes, it's an impulse purchase. Marketers and advertisers certainly try to capitalize on our tendency to purchase things on an impulse to increase the profit from each transaction.

For example, a sale. You see an item that you don't really need right now, don't even want to buy, didn't even plan to buy... but since it is being offered at a flat 50% discount, you buy it. You rationalize to yourself, "I'll use this in a couple of months."

The truth is that you could have done without that extra pair of jeans, or that set of cufflinks. You certainly already had more than you need and can use regularly.

Other times, it's just a lack of willpower.

You walk by a dozen bakeries on your way to work everyday. You have resolved to yourself that until such time as you lose those extra 15 pounds that you have put on over the last couple of years, you won't so much as step inside a bakery, lest you be tempted by the glazed toppings of the fresh, aromatic, delicious looking processed foods.

But over time, your willpower depletes. You partied hard one night, and then the following morning, you woke up late... and realized you had a terrible hangover. You get ready quickly, but in your haste, you spill a cup of coffee over your only well ironed shirt. So now you have to put on that smelly disgusting shirt to office that you wore yesterday.

As soon as you step inside the office, your boss starts yelling at you because you are late. Even though you skipped breakfast, and didn't have anything other than a cup of coffee, you still couldn't get to the office on time owing to the terrible traffic jam along the way.

As the day progresses, it just continuously seems to get worse. Your sister calls you up asking for some monetary help. She needs to "borrow" a sum of $2000 from you which she promises to return as soon as she realistically can. But, she tells you, if you don't "lend" it to her, her life will end up being in total disarray.

Of course, you know that "lending" to her means essentially just giving her the $2000.

At this point of time you are quite hungry, thirsty, and even have a bladder that seems to be on the verge of exploding. In the hopes of impressing your boss with your superior work ethic, you have been inside your room for the last 4 hours, and now you realize you haven't once urinated in the last seven hours.

So you get angry at her, and tell her to mind her own affairs herself. She cries and yells back at you, and your mood is completely soured.

You decide to skip lunch because you are already behind the schedule on your project. You work hard, but as the day progresses, you continue to get grumpier and grumpier.

By the evening, you are ready to fly off the handle just as soon as someone would wish a "Good Evening" to you.

And you are now hungry, angry, tired, have bloated eyes with a burning sensation in them, and feeling pretty bad about screaming at your sister. You decide to call her up and patch up things with her first thing you reach home.

But right now, you are just so very hungry.

And at this time, you see across the street a stunning looking bakery with delicious breads and pastries on display.

You know you are not supposed to go in there. But to hell with all that right now. Right now you are pissed at life, not thinking straight, and need food. You need gratification and you need it now. You have held back long enough.

Before you know it, you are already inside the bakery. You find your hand automatically reaching for your wallet and drawing out a crisp $20 bill to buy the most exquisite looking little cake in the shop.

Who has the time for cooking a salmon steak?

While this example is extreme, this also illustrates that the person with even the greatest will power reserves will sometimes find himself or herself in a situation where their willpower runs out... and they compromise.

Luckily, both these traits can be handled with some training. We'll talk more about the solutions in a while.

Wired for Immediate Gratification

Back in the day, if you came across a fruit, there would be no sense in storing it. Someone could steal it from your house when you were away hunting. And even if that did not happen, it would rot on its own in just a couple of days. You didn't have refrigerators back then, did you?

So it would make perfect sense to consume it right away.

In fact the people who consumed fast, and in larger quantities, had a definitive advantage as far as survival was concerned.

As such, human beings are wired to consume instantly.

Like I said before, we haven't yet made the connection that money is not as perishable as a banana, for instance. Not on an instinctive level.

So as soon as you have money, you tend to want to consume it.

Instant gratification might have been a survival advantage in the caveman days. But today, delayed gratification is what makes or breaks your future.

Be it health, wealth, or relationships... delaying gratification always has its rewards. Waiting for the right time to consume is the most common trait in almost all successful people.

Your IQ doesn't matter as much as your ability to delay gratification. Your academic qualifications don't matter nearly as much. Your talents don't matter nearly as much. Your looks certainly don't matter as much.

When it comes to predicting success, the ability of a person to delay gratification is the greatest indicator.

This ability to delay gratification is also known as will power.

So let's talk about what will power is, how you can understand it, and maximize it in order to maximize your chance for succeeding in life.

Imagine a container of oil. This is your willpower reserve.

This container is filled with your willpower. Your willpower is the oil that fills this tank.

Every time you have a good night's sleep, you refill your tank to the brim.

As you go through the day, every time you make a rational decision and go against your instinctive desires, you spend a little oil.

Every time you get angry but suppress your anger, you puncture a little hole in your tank. A similar thing happens when you are anxious.

Basically, every time you use your willpower, you lose a little bit of it. Quite logical, right?

Every time you consume something like coffee or

sugar that makes you hyperactive and energetic at once, and then makes you feel like you just crashed and burned, you consume a significant portion of oil in your tank.

As you continue to run out of oil (willpower) you begin to lose virtually all control over yourself. You start following your instincts, and you stop listening to your rational brain.

Of course, your rational brain is often at odds with your instinctive desires. Rationally, you may want to avoid spending money on things that you don't need, but your instinct compels to spend resources and when your willpower deteriorates, you stop listening to your rational mind, and start following your instincts blindly.

This applies not just to your spending habits, by the way. It also applies to other habits that have a huge impact on your life.

For people trying to cut down on smoking or drinking, every time they resist the urge, they use up some of their will power. If their willpower reserve (tank) runs low, they end up smoking another cigarette or buying a Jack Daniels.

For others, seeking attention and sex from the opposite sex might become an unhealthy habit.

As you can see, your will power is your first line of defense against all your base desires that harm your life in today's world. In fact, it is also your only defense against your own instinctive tendencies that keep you broke, unhealthy, and in unhappy relationships in life.

And as such, it is also the greatest predictor of your

success or failure in life, over the long term.

Naturally, you should do everything in your power to prevent your willpower reserve from getting depleted.

And here are some of the habits that you must form, that will help you in your quest to become not only wealthy, but also healthy, attractive, and satisfied.

First things first.

You need adequate sleep. If you don't sleep at least six to seven hours every night (or day, in some cases, although you'd do well to avoid that sort of a lifestyle) your willpower reserve won't be fully refilled.

Which means you will have less willpower to play with throughout the day.

Consequently, you will be prone to run out of it rather quickly. And then it's back to unhealthy eating, spending, and other disastrous habits.

 So get enough sleep.

Secondly, you need to learn to handle your stress better. Stress is basically anything on the spectrum of anger to anxiety.

Dealing With Stress

I'll give you a quick explanation of how stress works and how to deal with it.

Anger is caused by hurt. You hurt when you have unmet needs. These needs may be physical, emotional or psychological. For instance, if someone disrespects you, or insults you, your need for respect might be compromised. That would hurt you, and cause you to be angry.

Anxiety is similar. Only anxiety is caused by loss (or a fear of it.) For instance, you have a large bill coming in, but you don't have the money in your bank account right now. That would cause anxiety, right?

Every kind of stress you can imagine is a mixture of anger and anxiety. Every kind of stress you can experience.

Now, there are healthy ways to deal with stress, and there are unhealthy ways to deal with stress. But before I talk about those, I need to talk about something that can prevent stress from entering your system in the first place.

Let's use a simple analogy.

In chemistry, acids and alkaline substances neutralize each other. This process is known as acid-base titration. So let's say you take an equal number of molecules of hydrochloric acid, and of sodium hydroxide (an alkaline solution.)

If you mix these together, you will immediately witness an acid base titration. In other words, the acid and base will neutralize each other. And you will be left with just water and (sodium chloride which is also the) common salt that we consume.

That is the nature of a titration.

Now imagine, what if you had something to titrate anger with? And what if you had something inside your cybernetic system to neutralize anxiety with?

'Wouldn't it be love-r-ly?' (I hope you didn't miss that reference!)

Well, the good news, is that you do. You do have psychological countermeasures for both anxiety and anger.

For anxiety, the neutralizing agent is something called confidence. That's right, confidence.

Confidence and anxiety can literally never co-exist. If you have more confidence than anxiety, then your confidence might get eroded a bit when a fear of loss enters your system... but in the end, confidence will win out, and you won't feel anxious. Maybe less confident, but not anxious.

In the previous example, where you had a large bill coming to you, but no money - imagine you had the ability to walk into a client's office and get them to sign a check for you.

You have complete faith that this is doable, because throughout your career you have done it hundreds of times. You are confident that you can do it again.

Would you feel anxious?

Of course not.

So if you have enough confidence, you'll never feel anxious.

Now, let's talk about anger. Remember how anger stems from a feeling of hurt. And hurt is nothing more than (real or perceived) loss of well-being.

In other words, you feel angry when you feel you have unmet needs.

The natural neutralizing agent for anger is well-being.

If you have a lifestyle where you have extreme levels of well-being, would you feel angry?

Let's take an example.

Let's say that your mother is visiting you from out of town. And as usual, she has been nagging and complaining about a million things that she thinks you are doing wrong in life.

Then, your salary has been delayed this month. Your boss said that you'd not be paid before the eighth day of the month, so you are about to run out of cash any day now, and rent is overdue. So are the bills.

Your girlfriend (or boyfriend) has also been acting a bit strange. You suspect they might be having an affair.

You feel hungry, and so you go down to the local supermarket to grab a sandwich before you go to work. You are getting late, but there's a fifteen minute queue.

When finally you reach the checkout counter, the cashier is rude and angry, and disrespectfully tells you to go back and get the sandwich weighed from someone else.

At this point, would you be feeling angry?

I, for one, would not blame you for flying off the handle.

Why?

Because your well-being is pretty low. You have far too many unmet needs. You have an unmet need for food, for money, for respect, for peace, for affection, for emotional security and you are also anxious about not being able to pay your bills on time.

And when the cashier disrespects you, you would have to be an unusually strong willed person not to feel angry.

On the other hand, consider this scenario.

What if you were Warren Buffet. Everywhere you go, people walk up to you with a big smile on their faces. You have a Billion Dollars available in cash right away, and your check can never be dishonored.

Your partner loves you, and hot young women are eyeing you all day long.

Your kids respect you. So do the people in your company, and everyone else you meet.

So you go to the supermarket (Why would Mr. Buffet go to a supermarket? Answer: Because this is my book, and even Mr. Buffet is subject to my wishes in these hypothetical scenarios) and the cashier is rude to you.

Would you feel angry now?

Of course not!

You'd feel a little sorry for the cashier herself. Maybe she's having a bad day. Maybe you could help her. Could you offer her a job?

Those would be your thoughts. Literally.

You would be able to alleviate her anger with a smile and a word of wisdom. Maybe even bring a ray of hope in what has obviously been a sad day to her so far.

So if you have well-being (in other words, your needs are being met) then you won't feel angry easily.

Anger and a state of well-being are matter and anti matter. They are acid and base. They titrate and neutralize each other.

So those are your natural psychological defenses against stress.

Now, there is another powerful defense against stress of any kind. This defense is the strongest protection that keeps anger, anxiety, and anything in between out of your mind.

It is also what brings you respect and admiration from other people.

It's called having strong boundaries.

"Give me the courage to change what I can, and to ignore what I can't, and the wisdom to know the difference."

This is one of the most profound prayers I have heard, and used in my life.

There are some things that you can do, and there are other things that you can't. There are some things in your control, and then there are other things that aren't.

If you understand the difference between those two

categories, virtually all stress can be eliminated.

For instance, you can control what you do with your time right now. And what you buy with your money.

You can't control what someone else does with their time or money.

You can control what time you leave for work. But you can't control the amount of traffic on the road. A wise man once called that "God's Business, and not mine."

So here's the source of all stress...

Trying to control things that are outside your boundaries. That is what causes stress.

So for instance, if you make an offer to a potential client, and they say no, and then you take that rejection personally, or let that rejection hamper you by affecting your emotions, then you have weak boundaries.

See, making an offer to someone is within your boundaries, and within your control. Accepting or rejecting that offer is their business, not yours.

If you find yourself saying something along the lines of "He should have done this" or "She should have chosen that product" then you have boundary issues.

You might have control over other people's actions, though. If you are the CEO of a company, you certainly have some degree of control over what people in your company do. And you can create conditions to enforce that control.

So you might say, "We are focusing on this project right now, and I want all of you to bring these thirty clients in over the next sixty days." Failure to comply would mean that they would be risking getting suspended or fired from the job.

But that's influence.

As your influence grows, you gain the ability to direct and lead other people.

Still, the most fundamental thing you control are your resources, your time & effort, and your rights.

You have a right to start a business. You have the right to play a video game instead of doing that. What you do is entirely up to you.

You can do anything in life as long as you are willing to accept the consequences.

Yes, you can even go and try to rob someone at a gun point, or do even worse. But there would be consequences for that. The society has procedures to punish that sort of action. If you can live with the punishment, by all means do it.

In case it isn't clear, the author (aka me) is not recommending that you go out and rob someone.

All I am saying is that whatever you do with your time, your resources and your effort is within your control, and within your boundaries.

Make the right decisions, and your sphere of influence increases. Society rewards you with greater influence over other people's actions and resources.

Make the wrong decisions (like playing video games all day long, or worse robbing someone) and the society will punish you. And your boundaries will shrink, and your sphere of influence will decrease.

What Are Good Boundaries Like?

Good boundaries are like a good immigration department. They open up to good, honest and worthy individuals, and remain closed to the "bad" people.

So, for instance, if your boss wants you to focus on acquiring and developing relationship on a personal level with a high quality prospect, then they are exerting their influence over you. Now, you get to decide if you are going to open up your boundaries to the boss.

In this case, you most likely will because it is a good use of your time and effort.

On the other hand, if your boss wanted you to "cook the books", so to speak, a wise decision would be to close your boundaries to him, and say NO.

In fact, the consequence of saying NO to such a request might be getting fired from that company. But honestly, why would you want to stay employed at such a dysfunctional company anyway?

Let's take another example.

If your significant other is opening up their heart to you for intimacy, the best decision you can make is to open your boundaries to them, and to let them in.

But when the same person makes an unjustified demand of you, you'd be wise to close your boundaries to them temporarily, and to deny them access to your time, money, effort, or other resources.

This is the hallmark of a healthy relationship. Healthy relationships are a consequence of healthy boundaries.

You open up your boundaries to them when they are being constructive and affectionate, helping you get your needs met while theirs get met too. You allow them access to your heart, emotions, body, money, time and resources.

Yet if the same person misuses those privileges, or starts acting destructively you immediately withdraw those privileges. You close your boundaries to them until such time as they start behaving properly and constructively again.

So those are the boundary functions.

If you have strong boundaries, you will literally never feel anger or anxiety ever again. No one will be able to make you do what you do not want to do. No one will be able to force you to make decisions that you don't feel are in your best interest.

Once you realize that lending $2000 to your sister is your prerogative, and it is also well within your boundaries to deny her request... and that if she cannot handle that rejection it is her problem not yours, you will be able to gain enormous self-respect.

In fact, even your sister will eventually respect you for standing your ground and making a wise decision that taught her the value of saving money for the rainy days.

So if someone else gets angry and says something disrespectful to you... if you have strong boundaries, you will realize that it is within their boundaries to say whatever they want with their mouth. What is inside YOUR boundaries to either throw that person out of your life forever, or temporarily... or to file a formal complaint against them if they are an employee at a place of business where you are a patron, or to assertively and strongly, yet politely tell them something along the lines of, "You will not talk to me like that again. I want you to apologize to me for disrespecting me. I treat you with respect and I need to be treated with respect. Please apologize and tell me that you will never talk to me insultingly ever again."

All these things are within your boundaries.

Stop focusing on what others should have said, or not said, or done, or not done. And start focusing on your actions.

Which brings me to the last section of this segment...

How To Use Your Boundaries To Increase Well-Being & Confidence

When you are angry, you can do three things.

The first thing you can do is to suppress your anger. Every time you do that, you destroy your well-being. And you store up what is commonly known as depression.

That's right.

Depression is nothing but anger suppressed

repeatedly.

Often depressed men and women are people who pride themselves in that they never getting angry.

No pill of any kind will ever cure depression permanently. The only permanent cure for depression is well-being. Having all your needs met, and using your boundaries properly to deal with depression.

The next thing you can do with your anger is channel it into random aggression. Also known as "flying off the handle."

Often, it is possible to hurt other people with your anger, because most people have poor boundaries. If you get aggressive, most people will most often fail to recognize that you getting angry is none of their business, and that your anger doesn't hurt them in the least, unless they allow it by letting their boundaries remain opened to you.

So for instance, if you get aggressive with me, I'll simply either have you removed from my office or home, or walk out if I don't have that within my control. That's me closing my boundary to an aggressive person.

But even though most people have weak boundaries and will take your aggression personally and emotionally... and continue to engage with your aggression instead of shutting it out, sooner or later it will backfire on you.

How?

Well, aggression often begets aggression, right?

So if you push me, and I have weak boundaries, I

might push back, leading to escalation of a physically violent nature.

This will cause you to feel even more hurt, and consequently, you'll feel angrier.

This leads to a negative spiral that ends very badly for either both of us, or at least you.

So if suppressing anger causes depression, and at the same time getting aggressive causes a negative spiral that hurts you even more, how do you deal with anger, if it does manage to get inside your system?

The Answer: Through Assertiveness

You assert your needs.

You realize that you, and only you are responsible for your well being. Only you were put on the face of this planet to get your needs met. Especially when you are an adult. You can't rely on others to help you meet your needs.

Therefore, you channel your anger into assertiveness.

If someone disrespects you, you assertively yet coolly tell them, "Do not talk to me that way again. Please apologize to me now." If they don't comply, you move them out of your life. That's how you use your boundaries.

If your boss pays you too little for too long hours, you assertively yet politely ask for a pay raise. If they refuse, you find a better job for yourself, and quit this one. In that order.

You get the idea.

The correct way to use anger is to channel it into assertiveness. Use the anger to get your needs met.

As this happens, your well-being increases.

You see more of your needs start getting met, and eventually, you don't get angry very easily.

Combine a state of well-being with proper boundary exertions, as well as channeling anger into assertion instead of raw aggression or suppressing it so that it becomes depression.

And that is how you deal with anger.

Now let's move to anxiety.

If you fear losing something, but do nothing with it, you tend to become erratic. Irritated and prone to addictions. People who become alcoholics, drug addicts, smoking addicts, binge eaters, big spenders, spendthrifts, "thin skinned" etc. are people who are anxious about certain things in life, but do nothing to deal with the anxiety.

Then there is the negative way to deal with anxiety. Blame it on someone else. Become the victim.

Since other people often have weak boundaries, they will often readily accept your blame, and accept your victim frame.

But self victimization sooner or later backfires, just like aggression does. Eventually, people get fed up and start cutting you out of their lives, at best, and retaliating with anger and aggression, at worst.

Then there is the other issue that blaming someone else for your losses or fear of loss, and playing victim does not really take care of the problem at hand. If anything, it creates a negative spiral that becomes increasingly hard for you to dig yourself out of.

The best way to deal with anxiety is simple... ACTION.

Just act.

Worried about money? Sit down and create a plan to make money. Then act. Immediately.

Worried about relationships? Sit down and talk to the people who form these relationships with you. Then make the right decisions rationally. Sometimes, that decision can be letting go of a relationship.

Worried about your health? Eat a nutritious meal, and go lift weights in the gym.

Anxiety is easily relieved. Action is the antidote.

This action creates experience and positive references. Basically, it creates more confidence for you.

You should recall that anxiety is undone by confidence.

So the next time you feel anxious, remember that that anxiety is a ticket for you to create confidence. How? By taking action. Making decisions and taking action.

So that brings us to the conclusion of this section.

By now, you have enough tools to deal with the two

forces of nature that keep you broke, unhealthy and out of control, namely anxiety and anger.

The more you use your anger to act assertively and increase your well-being... and the more you use your anxiety to take actions and build confidence, the less will power you will dissipate in dealing with stress.

Now let's go back to discussing will power.

You will recall that we were discussing how to keep your will power reserve (tank) from running out of oil (will power) too quickly.

Here are some other best practices:

Don't eat sugars and don't drink coffee. These things give you an instant surge of energy, but they also lead to an inevitable crash of energy levels in a few hours.

These energy crashes drain our will power.

So if you get a craving for something sweet, eat a fruit.

Don't allow yourself to get hungry enough that you'll eat anything that you can get your hands on. Have proper meals, that are delicious and nutritious. Fine meats, raw veggies for carbs, and fruits for sweets. Snack on nuts instead of chocolates or chips.

Nutritious foods not only make you look good and make you stronger and healthy, but also they don't cause energy crashes that drain your will power.

If you are filled, and are not hungry, the temptation those pastries held previously will just disappear.

Your will power is a limited commodity.

It's scarce. You want to use it well.

The best way to use your will power is to harness it to inculcate new healthy habits.

For instance, your will power is highest right after a good night of sleep.

So if you don't regularly go to the gym, your will power will be best used by joining a gym, and then just using brute force will power to get yourself to the gym every morning for a month.

Do this without fail, and you will find that you have a new habit. Suddenly, not going to the gym will feel unnatural, and you won't require will power to go to the gym anymore.

You also want to use will power to protect yourself from making bad choices like spending money on things you don't need. Of course, every time you use your will power, you deplete your reserve by a tiny amount.

But overtime, using will power has a very good effect.

Just like your muscles grow when subjected to external stress, your will power reserve also grows when subjected to external temptations.

Every time you use your will power to curb your baser instincts that are prone to lead you astray, your tank becomes larger. Your will power reserve becomes deeper.

Over the long term, as you keep practicing the use of

your will power, your will power reserve grows.

This means, you will not run out of will power as easily as you run out of it today.

There are other ways to train your will power reserve, and to grow it. These ways are scientifically proven, and I recommend a book called the Willpower Instinct by Kelly McGonigal. It's an excellent book that goes into greater depths of the subject matter of will power.

But here are a few suggestions:

Exercise regularly. Weight lifting helps grow the will power reserve over the long term.

Practice your will power regularly. Regularly make the rational decision when your baser instincts direct you towards instant gratification. Not only does it strengthen your will power reserve, but it also makes you feel more alive. I can personally vouch for both these effects. Every time I make the right decision, I feel completely alive, present and in the moment, ready to deal with the world.

Correct diet and optimum sleep hours are also linked to will power.

As you can see, will power is a matter of life-style. The better your overall lifestyle is, the more cultivated your will power reserve will be. And as a consequence you will achieve even greater successes, allowing you to have an even better lifestyle.

Of course, don't let me give you the impression that always curbing your instincts is the right way to go. It's definitely not.

Every once in a while, you can rationally make a choice to eat a cheese-burst pizza followed by a really sweet, sugary cheesecake. It's fine, and as long as you rationally permit yourself to do things like this, while understanding the consequences, there is nothing wrong in allowing your instincts a temporary free reign.

Not only is it allowable, but also recommendable.

If you want to spend money, and you have disposable money after you have made your investments for the year, and saved enough for the rainy day, and put aside enough to cover your living expenses... there is no reason why you shouldn't spend.

The important thing is that your rational mind should permit you to engage in such activities, and then it's fine.

VALUE

So now we move to the more interesting part of wealth creation.

How do you become wealthy?

Before we answer that question, let us examine what wealth really means. You will be surprised to know that cash is not equivalent to wealth.

I am going to explain it to you, and then talk about how to create wealth for yourself, as well as for others around you, while at the same time creating wealth for your nation as well as the entire world.

So what is wealth?

Well, wealth is an accumulation of objects and rights, tangible and intangible, that provide and deliver value to you, as well as other human beings.

So for instance, if you have a coffee shop that provides value to your patrons then that is wealth.

Now, keep in mind that value is not just the tangible value that is most often thought of as value. For instance, a coffee shop is not valuable just because it provides coffee. It also provides a warm (or cool if it's hot out) place to sit and rest, and to talk to friends, family and business associates. That is the intangible value.

Starbucks takes it one step further. Of course they sell coffee, and of course they sell a comfortable lounging place, but they also sell a certain amount of prestige. Just because they charge $5, or even $8 for a cup of coffee, a vast majority of people on the planet can not afford to sit and have coffee at Starbucks.

For this reason, frequenting Starbucks is also a status symbol. So a feeling of significance is the emotional value that is sold at Starbucks. This is reflected in the way the staff at Starbucks treat you.

Many patrons will purposely and deliberately take it one step further. They will treat Starbucks as though it's a place that is beneath them. They look at sitting and spending time at Starbucks with disdain. This is deeply psychological and subconscious of course. No one consciously does that, or enunciates these emotions. They take the whole significance thing a whole degree further by simply buying coffee, and then walking out. Here's what they are sub communicating to others as well as to themselves...

"I don't have the time to sit down here. I am too busy for that. I am too important for that. And of course $8 does not sound too steep to me for a cup of coffee. It's still a commodity to me. I don't need the ambience and the lounging facilities to make it worth my eight bucks. I wouldn't even dream of buying that coffee across the block that sells for 50 cents a cup."

Essentially, they are addicted to the feeling of significance. Of course, Starbucks as a "for profit" organization is only too happy to oblige.

And that illustrates my concept beautifully.

Wealth is anything that creates value for other people.

Let's say you have an apartment in the middle of a bustling city with tons of jobs around, like the Manhattan Island in New York.

This apartment is a kind of wealth, because many people would be willing to pay a significant amount of their salaries in order to live there and call the apartment their home.

The apartment goes to the highest bidder around in most cases, and the more buyers there are, the higher it goes for. It can be sold, or rented. Either way, it's a form of wealth because it has great utility.

In general, the higher the scarcity of availability, the higher the prices of that kind of wealth will be. Whether someone wants to own it permanently, or just temporarily, if they can derive value from it, they'll pay as much as they need to.

So what is value?

To illustrate the meaning of value, let's take an example.

Let me ask you a question. How much can you sell a cheeseburger for?

Two Dollars? Five? Ten?

How about fifty?

Can you sell a cheeseburger for fifty bucks?

What about $500? Is it possible to sell it for $500? Maybe you think you can't. But I can.

In fact, I can even sell it for one Million Dollars.

That's right. I can sell one cheese burger for a Million cool bucks.

How, you ask, in disbelief.

Allow me to elaborate.

Let's say a private jet crashes in the middle of the Saharan desert, and the wealthy jet setter miraculously escapes without a scratch. Except, he doesn't know which way to go, has no food or water, and in just two short days, is on the verge of dying.

If I went to him and sold him a bottle of water, a cheese burger and a set of directions to get out of there for a Million Dollars, do you think this multi millionaire would hesitate in signing me a Million Dollar check?

Of course not.

And that example (which I gratefully borrowed from the late Mr. Gary Halbert, the Prince of Print advertising) illustrates the concept of value.

Value Is Relative

How much is anything worth?

It depends on a bunch of factors:

1.   How commonly available is it? If it is scarce, it tends to be of higher value.

2.   How many people want it, and are competing for it? The larger the "target audience" for any item is relative to the supply ability of the seller(s) the higher the prices will be.

3.   How much do they need it, want it, crave it, or desperately need it urgently?

4.   How much money have they got?

Take those things into account, and you have a pretty good idea about how much something is valued at.

Luckily, most markets and industries today have matured to a point where the demand and supply curves have stabilized, at least temporarily. This allows us to know how much to pay for something as a buyer of value, and how much we can charge for something as a seller.

If I try to charge $20,000 a month for a studio apartment in New York City today (in 2014) it's highly likely that no one would ever rent my apartment.

Consequently, if I try to charge $200 a month for it, I might get a lot of takers, and it would be leased out rather quickly, maybe even in an hour of listing it at that price, but then I'd lose out on all the money I could have made.

So I look around and find that people are willing to pay $1500 to $2000 for an apartment like mine in the same neighborhood, and so I can also charge $2000 a moth for it.

It might take a month or two before someone leases the apartment, but I'd end up making far more money than I'd have made if I had underpriced my apartment.

Again, desperate times call for desperate measures.

So if a European tourist needed to rent my apartment for just a month, and found that there are not too many apartments around that can be rented for less than $5000, and that living in a comparable serviced apartment or hotel would cost them $300 a day (that's $9000 a month), then they'd be more than happy to pay me $4000 for the same apartment.

The simplest way to be able to charge as much money as you want to charge is formulaic:

1.   Find a desperate, or irrationally passionate group of people who are looking for a solution to some problem. This group of people is called "target audience."

2.   These people must be able (aka they must be wealthy, or at least affluent) and willing to pay for whatever you want to sell to them. The definitive proof that they'll buy from you is that they've already bought something similar from another company in the past at a similarly high enough price point.

3.   Ensure that they are great enough in number. And that they are easy and economic to reach. If it costs you $100 in advertising to deliver your message to one person in your target audience, then you have either a bad marketing method, or a bad market.

4. Observe their greatest frustrations and dissatisfactions with the current products and services available on the marketplace. Really study them and find their pain points. The easiest way to identify these pain points is to read their reviews of existing best selling products or services.

5. Create a product or service that deals with the pain that your target audience is having. In this way, you create a distinctive product or service that caters to their innate needs and wants like no other product or service on the market.

6. Advertise your offer to them as cost effectively as possible, and as regularly as you can afford to. How you do this is beyond the scope of this book, and so is the message contained in your advertisement.

This is how you go about creating value.

Now, money is valuable to people. If you think people don't like money, try begging. You will realize how difficult it is to get just 50 cents from someone's pocket.

On the other hand, it is rather easy and straightforward to sell $50 Million mansions and private jets.

Why?

Because the buyers of those $50 Million jets are getting something in return for their money. And whatever they are getting is more valuable to them than the Fifty Million Dollars sitting in their bank accounts.

In a few minutes we will talk more about what people value, want and crave. And consequently pay for. But first, understand this principle...

If you want someone to pay you a sum of ten thousand dollars, give them something that they perceive more valuable than their ten thousand dollars.

If you want to charge people a Million Dollars for your services, build up your aura, reputation, portfolio and case studies where being able to spend time with you, and availing your services becomes worth more than a Million Dollars to people in your target audience.

For a Multi-Millionaire dying in the Saharan desert, his life is worth way more than one Million Dollars I'd charge him for a bottle of water and a cheese burger. Because I am not really selling a cheese burger. I am actually selling his life back to him. And if all he had was a Million Dollars, it would still be worth it for him to buy his life from me. He'd be happy to stay alive.

Everybody's life is worth more to them than their bank balance, right?

Please note that we are not discussing the ethics of pricing and selling here. We are merely discussing the psychological and economic aspects of how value exchanges take place.

To me, the burger and the bottle of water was worth way less than $1 Million. But to the millionaire, it was his life.

The higher the differential in value, the easier the

trade.

I have a grand total of $62,000 sitting in my bank account right now. I'd happily spend it for an evening with Warren Buffet if I got an opportunity to pick his brains and get a photograph with him... maybe even a testimonial from him about how I really understand the nature of investments far better than almost every person on this planet, excepting a few!

That testimonial, that photograph, and that evening of philosophical discussion is worth way more than $62,000 to me. And if I had $6.2 Million in my bank account, I'd happily spend that too.

Because a testimonial from him, or even just a photograph with him would help me sell a thousand times more rapidly and more authoritatively than I do right now.

The value of that testimonial and photograph would be that it would instantly get me many Millions of Dollars in sales.

Not to mention, the change in mindset and thinking would enable me to cut down on many years of hard learning.

And that is worth way more than all that I have right now.

Since the value differential is high, I'd pay money easily.

On the other hand, I'd be averse to giving someone even $100 if I don't think I am getting fair value in exchange. I just wouldn't.

And that is how human beings are.

Which brings me to the evaluation of the next principle relevant to this discussion...

PSYCHOLOGICAL JUSTICE MECHANISM

Can anyone say NO to free money?

Let me allow an experiment that has been repeated in many different circumstances and forms all over the world.

The experiment was as follows...

Two people were taken into a room simultaneously.

Person A was given told that they would be given $100, and that they had to split it between themselves and another Person B sitting in the next room.

They could choose to split the $100 any way they liked. They could keep just $20, or they could decide they wanted $80.

Person B couldn't change the split, they could only say YES or NO.

The catch was that Person B had the right to veto. So

if Person B didn't like the deal, they could say NO to it. And if they said NO, nobody would get anything. But if they said YES, they would be accepting the split that Person A had decided.

This experiment was repeated many times with many different pairs of anonymous people who didn't know each other at all.

So here are the results of this experiment:

Whenever Person A (who decides the way $100 would be split) chose $50 or less for themselves, Person B would invariably say YES.

When Person A decided they wanted $60, and Person B would get only $40, in most cases Person B still said YES. But some said NO.

When Person A decided they wanted $70 for themselves leaving only $30 for Person B, in almost 70% of the cases, person B said NO.

Imagine that!

People said NO to free money.

Why? Because they perceived that they were being treated with injustice. "Why should he get $70 when I get only $30?"

And that in a nutshell is the psychological justice mechanism.

Whenever we perceive that injustice is being done to us, we want to cancel that activity or trade.

This mechanism also keeps us poor.

See, this mechanism makes trade incredibly difficult.

The easiest way to get a lot of people to pay you a lot of money is by delivering something to them that is of far more value to them than their money.

So for instance, if you have $50,000 and I offer you something that you perceive is worth $200,000... it'd be a piece of cake for me to sell it to you.

However, most people don't want to trade like this. They believe in what they call a "fair" trade. $50,000 in exchange for $50,000 worth of stuff.

This mindset is natural. It's the same psychological justice mechanism that I just spoke about. But it salso keeps them poor, and keeps them away from wealth.

Remember: The fastest way to create wealth for yourself is to let other people have what they value more than money.

Of course, money is not wealth, as we will soon discuss. But it is a tool that is necessary to create wealth. Without money, you can't create wealth, unless you are really creative.

Which brings me to my next point.

At this point, you will want to go over to www.lakshaybehl.com/wealth-gifts and claim your free gifts. One of the free gifts is a tiny little black book of business ideas that allow you to gain control of other people's wealth. This is of course just one of the many gifts that you get. I will talk about the other gifts as we move along.

To conclude, understand that if you are going to become very wealthy very quickly, you are going to let other people get the larger share of the profits generated from any deal.

The key here is that you are going to be the one person who will leverage other people's wealth to the maximum extent possible, and benefit enormously, while creating enormous benefits for others too.

The little black book of ideas shows you seven extremely simple to implement and neat ways in which you can create wealth for yourself and others even if you have absolutely nothing to your name right now.

Here's a hint: A ton of people out there have resources that can potentially be valuable to you, but are useless to them. Why? Because they don't have either the time or the inclination to use them.

Think about this... How many underutilized resources do you have right now?

See most people have underutilized assets. If you need something, simply go out and find someone who has that particular resource, but are underutilizing it, and do a Joint Venture deal with them. Here's what you say to them...

"Dear Mr. X

You are currently in possession of Y. I am in need of Y. I notice that you are underutilizing Y. You only use it from 8 AM to 6 PM.

If you allow me to use your Y from 6 PM to 10 PM, I will give you 25% of all my profits generated from the activities related to Y.

This will help you expediently recover the sunk investment you have in your Y, and I won't have to buy Y for myself.

If this sounds interesting to you, give me a call at xxx.

We'll sit down to work out the details.

It's a win-win situation.

Yours truly

Lakshay Behl"

Now, don't let the psychological justice mechanism keep you from doing this deal.

Sure, if you spend the money, you won't have to give up 25% of your profits to anyone, and over the long term, that would be more beneficial to you.

But more often than not, you will find yourself lacking enough cash to be able to buy everything that you need in order to do everything that you need to do in order to turn your vision into reality.

So Joint Venture with someone who has the resources that you need, and you are on the fast track to creating leveraged wealth with zero downside.

What's the worst thing that can happen in this example?

If you make zero dollars in profit, you owe your partner nothing. At least you haven't spent anything, right? What if you had spent valuable cash capital buying stuff that wouldn't benefit you at the end of the day?

The ideal thing to do is to go out, and get other people to give you their underutilized resources so that you can leverage their investment at zero risk to you. You may be left with only 10% of the profits at the end of the day, but you spent as little money as you possibly could, and it's all pure profit.

ABUNDANCE

Most people live in a world of scarcity.

As a consequence, most people operate from a position of fear. In fact, the psychological justice mechanism that we discussed in the previous section was a natural consequence of the scarcity mindset.

I touched upon scarcity in Section 1.

Our ancestors truly lived in a world of scarcity. There just weren't enough resources to go around. There was insufficient food, and there was insufficient land for everyone to get the best parts.

It's not as if they had modernized agriculture or skyscrapers, right?

So they lived in a world where valuable resources were scarce. As such, they fought for their fair share, and sometimes more. They would fight and kill other human beings for resources, because this meant greater chance of survival and replication for them and their family members.

But today, the world has changed.

See today, we have more than enough food for everyone. And we have clean and fresh water for every one. We are now at a point in our evolution where realistically every human being can be clothed like Solomon every day for the rest of their lives and there would still be too much fabric left over.

We have skyscrapers that reach hundreds of stories above the ground. So a one square kilometer piece of land effectively provides 100 square kilometers of housing space now.

We live in a world where there is too much stuff. We buy stuff we do not need. The world of scarcity just does not exist anymore.

Yet our metal wiring, our cybernetic system has not evolved to a point where we instinctively understand that we live in a world of abundance.

Like I said, proof is in the pudding. Observe the psychological justice mechanism. People got so competitive that they said NO to free money just because someone else stood to gain more than they could gain themselves for what they perceived as an equal amount of effort.

The first thing you need to understand is that there is no correlation between the number of hours you spend working and the amount of wealth you accumulate.

Accumulating wealth is all about mindset, habits and

practices. That is what this entire course is about.

The second thing is that if you deliver $50 worth of value to someone, you will have absolutely no trouble charging them $20 for it. As long as you can produce that product or service for less than $20, and profit on the deal, you are in business.

This is the essence of capitalism.

Creating value. Adding value to the raw ingredients and resources that can be obtained cheaply, and creating products, services and other forms of deliverables that you can sell for a much more expensive price.

Then the free market decides whether they like your offer or not. Ironically, the more value you offer, the more likely your target audience is to buy from you.

I want to remind you at this point that value is relative, and not absolute. And value can be derived from intangible deliverable like emotional fulfillment just as much, and even more than it can be derived from the tangible deliverable. Recall the example of Starbucks previously discussed.

They key to creating a ton of wealth is understanding that you can create a lot of value for people.

How?

Through **innovation**. So for instance, if you find a way to treat itchy corn painlessly and eradicate it from the root immediately, then you have something that a lot of people suffering from itchy corn would pay good money for. Why? Because it would be valuable to them. Very often, a price cannot be put upon the value of health and vitality of a person. For a person who has been suffering from painful and itchy corn for months, a cure like that would be godsend.

Through **creativity**. So if you were to start a coffee shop where people could sit all day long and use the internet in exchange for a token amount of just $5, for instance... and pay for whatever they consume separately, then you'd have on your hands an offer that would be very lucrative to people like me who don't like sitting alone in an office to work.

I like to be around people when I work. The trouble is that my colleagues and staff keep coming up to me if I sit in the middle of my office with everyone else.

So I often find myself gravitating towards Starbucks. I can avail free internet, and the energy and the vibe of that place really makes my productivity flow. In fact, a large portion of this very course is being written at various Starbucks outlets across the continent as I move from one city to another.

Through **systems**. Look at McDonalds. The value they offer is clean and hygienic food, fast and cheap. They never promised the most delicious food ever. That's not what they do. They don't promise a blend of exotic ingredients that will spoil your tastebuds in such a manner that you refuse to eat anything less delicious ever again in your life.

But the way they are able to create this value for such a

little price is by utilizing the power of systems.

Everything at a McDonald's outlet is systematized. How a particular product is to be created, how orders are to be taken, and even how staff is to be hired and trained. There is a system for everything. This systemization process ensures a uniformly high quality of service and product across the thousands of McDonalds outlets around the world.

Through **sheer arbitrage**. You buy raw materials. You invest capital in equipment. Then you employ people to turn that raw material into something that is quantifiably far more valuable than the raw material itself... where the whole is greater than the sum of its parts.

Case in point - Swiss Watch. Made out of metal. But far more valuable than just metal. It's precise. It's stunning. It's heavy. It's prestigious. It's built not just by putting hours into the raw material, but also expertise. It's a machine.

People pay thousands of dollars for Swiss watches, and they will continue to do so long after most people stop wearing watches altogether.

Why?

Because a Swiss watch is a status symbol. It's a way for someone to declare that they are significant, and they treat themselves like an important person.

You won't believe the number of deals that a Swiss watch, a nice car, and an Armani suit get you until you put those on yourself.

People sometimes talk about how the next world war will be because of scarcity of clean drinking water. Others say it will be because of scarcity of oil and petrochemicals.

These people fail to realize something really important and essential.

True wealth is inside the minds of human beings.

You see, maybe we can't extract more coal and petroleum from the planet once we've exhausted the current reserves.

But one of us can certainly come up with a way to utilize literally hundreds of as yet unexploited sources of natural energy - like solar energy, the energy of the flowing wind, or waves or tides.

People often talk about how a lack of freshwater can be a triggering factor for the next world war. I think it's only a matter of time before someone comes up with a way to cheaply filter seawater into potable water. Once that technology is taken to a mass scale, and made available to every household at a reasonable price, there would be no shortage of freshwater, would there?

Essentially, as our collective knowledge bans become more exhaustive, and our naturally curious attitude continues to lead to more and more newer innovations, the future is looking brighter than today.

A few hundred years ago, there was no such thing as a light bulb. Look around today. How many electrically powered sources of light are you surrounded with today?

A hundred years ago, flying was something that human beings just did not do. Today, things have changed, haven't they?

As our knowledge bank improves, we will continue to find newer and better ways to make human lives easier, simpler and safer.

Consequently, there will be more value to deliver, and to exploit.

Yet, most people think in terms of scarcity.

"How am I going to pay this bill?"

"How will my kids go to college?"

"How will we drive around once we run out of petroleum reserves of the planet?"

Look at any news channel and they will tell how dire things are, and how much worse they are getting.

It never ceases to amaze me that news readers who constantly utilize newer technology to be able to deliver content to audiences faster, at a higher quality and a lower cost continue with their fear mongering.

If you are going to be wealthy, and I mean truly wealthy, understand this...

There is an abundance of everything you need in life. And of everything you can possibly want.

Once you adopt the abundance mentality, you stop focusing on how you can leech value, and instead start focusing on how you can deliver value to other people.

Once you start doing that, money and wealth naturally follow. Which brings me to the next topic of discussion in this course... The Strategy that naturally creates wealth for everyone.

THE POWERFUL STRATEGY
OF PRE-EMINENCE

In this section, I am going to give you a strategy that will literally change the way you seek to create wealth for yourself and for others.

But first, let me ask you a question.

How many times have you witnessed the following scenario:

Jazz is selling something to Dan. Or at least trying to. Jazz is trying to convince Dan that he should buy the product (or service) from her.

But Dan seems reluctant and withdrawn.

Jazz tries harder to sell to him, but instead finds that the harder she sells, the more she drives Dan away.

Dan was interested a few minutes ago, but now he

seems turned off.

Jazz has listed numerous features and benefits, and has tried virtually all the four different closing techniques she knows... but Dan is simply not buying. He's not buying her product, and he's not buying her speech either.

Have you ever seen something like this play out between a seller and a prospect?

Or worse, have you ever been in the seller's position where the more you tried to convince the prospect to buy, the more he or she receded away from you?

I am sure you have, at one point or another.

Even if you are not a sales person, and even if you have never sold a product or a service in your life... you still have sold something to someone, right?

Maybe it was during a job interview were you were trying to convince the interviewer that you are the best person they could hire.

Maybe it was during your dating life where you subtly tried to sell your plus points to someone you were attracted to.

Maybe you were selling an idea, or even a philosophy.

Maybe you were raising investment capital for a new venture like we do on a regular basis for our acquisitions.

At some point or another, we all sell.

Only, some people find it extremely hard to sell anything, while others find it extremely easy, fun and energizing to sell.

Did I Just Say Energizing?

Can Selling Be Energizing & Fun?

The answer is YES.

This section will show you how.

You see, the Strategy of pre-eminence makes it virtually impossible for you to not sell to someone who is the right fit for whatever it is that you are selling.

But here's the caveat...

You will never be able to sell to someone who does not need, want, or is not a good match for whatever it is that you are offering.

In other words...

You will only be able to sell your offer, or your idea to someone who has a need, or a desire, or is a good match for whatever you're offering.

The strategy of pre-eminence guarantees that you will sell to everyone who is right for your offer. And do it from a position of respect, value, prestige and authority. And have fun as you do it.

Ready?

It's Not Us Vs Them

A fundamental mistake most people make while selling, or pitching anything to anyone is this... They see the prospect as their foe.

They see the prospective customer as someone who's needless objections need to be overcome. Whose walls of defenses need to be brought down before the sale can be made.

People seem to think that they have a transactional relationship with their customers. Ideally, people want prospects who show up, pay the price, take the product or service, and go away without wasting much time or requiring much effort.

Clients, Not Customers

A customer is someone who buys a product or service from you, and has a transactional relationship.

A client is someone who is under your care, guidance and protection. You have a two way transformational relationship with your client.

If you stop treating people as prospects or customers, and instead treat everyone like a client, you are on the right track.

And this is the huge difference...

You educate a client.

You protect them from making mistakes that can harm them.

You look out for their best interests over the long term.

You point them to the best possible buying options, even if it means turning away business today, because you are not carrying what they ought to buy.

You make recommendations instead of pitches.

You have their best interest at heart.

Every meeting that they have with you is enlightening, educational and entertaining.

They look up to you as someone who will guide them authoritatively, and who they can trust to recommend the best course of action for them.

That is the kind of relationship you need to have.

Once that happens... once they see you as the pre-eminent, trusted, go-to advisor, your market share rapidly increases.

The client loyalty rate goes through the roof, and they wouldn't even dream of abandoning you in order to buy from your competitor.

You can command higher prices simply because you are the expert.

In fact, price is no longer their buying criteria. They don't buy something from a competitor just because it's cheap. They buy it from you because they respect you, are loyal to you, and trust you to help them make the best possible decision.

Your clients keep coming back to you over many years. As a consequence, each of your clients brings in far more money than the industry average or the norm.

And all that happens because you follow the strategy

of Pre-Eminence. Simply stated, the strategy of Pre Eminence is as follows:

Look out for the best long term interests of your clients. Put their interests ahead of your own self interests. And guide them towards the best possible decisions.

It's of course up to them to make the final decisions, but it is your moral imperative to make them aware of the best possible opportunities, as well as the consequences of various choices on their lifestyle over the short term as well as the long term.

That's it.

When you start following the strategy of pre-eminence, you are no longer in a hurry to sell.

The first thing you do is you ask a bunch of deep, probing questions that give you a good overview of what your client truly needs right now.

Many times, people don't even know what they need.

Based on your inspection, you then make the optimum suggestion, and contrast it against their chosen solution. You tell them the pros and cons of the best possible solution, and those of the solution that they think they want.

Your conversation becomes prescriptive in nature, instead of being "salesy" or "pitchy".

You stop trying to sell, and you start helping.

Your clients value a conversation with you even before they buy something. They understand hat just being with you is valuable.

You share your knowledge freely.

Now of course there are things that you will charge for. Maybe you are a consultant and you charge for detailed planning or strategy sessions. Maybe you are a doctor and you charge for making prescriptions.

That is perfectly alright.

The idea is that you put their best interests ahead of your own.

And that is when selling becomes fun.

Now, here's something you need to watch out for...

The Importance of the End User

If you work in a B2B environment and cater to businesses who then cater to the end users either directly, or through another layer of businesses... ask yourself this simple truth...

How would the end user benefit and gain value?

At the end of every supply chain, there is an end user who consumes the products or services being manufactured or constructed.

Treat the end user as your real client. Apply the strategy of pre-eminence first and foremost to them, and thereafter to your own clients.

Why?

Because a business thrives when the end users find it to be pre-eminent.

So if your client is a business owner who's company serves the end users... all your efforts and advice should be catered to your client in such a way that the interests of their clients (the end users) are being looked out for first and foremost.

When that happens, the end users become loyal clients of your client. When that happens, your client finds you to be his or her trusted advisor, and becomes a loyal client for life.

So always focus on the end user.

I once had a client who had a very good product. It was easy for me to sell my consulting services to them. In fact, they asked me to be their consultant.

Since I always offered advice that would, to the best of my knowledge and experience, help their business grow... they readily trusted me.

Except, their business catered to a market that was shrinking. And it was getting increasingly hard to reach those people.

If a market becomes hard to reach, and the end users continue to shrink in number, and continue to lose their desire for the product or service, then you can't really service them well, right?

Unfortunately, in my youthful arrogance, I overlooked this factor. And jumped into what seemed to me to be the simplest marketing campaign.

It turned out to be a disaster.

After spending nearly $7000 we realized that the campaign wasn't going anywhere. That the sales weren't picking up at all. And that it was probably time for us to shut down the campaign.

I had focused my attention on my client. But the well-being of their business depended upon their clients. Who did not really exist.

The market continues to shrink. Even the most established players don't cross a Million Dollar in sales in that market today. And it is getting increasingly difficult to provide value to the end user.

In such cases, even the best marketing mind on the planet can not revive a flailing company.

So always apply the strategy of pre-eminence not just to the person you are talking to, but to (most importantly) the end user who would be paying for the product or service in question.

If you look out for the best interests of your clients (and their clients too, if you cater to businesses) then selling becomes easier than drinking a cup of coffee and singing a song.

And that brings me to the next section that is going to surprise you, and perhaps even shock you.

It goes against everything you might have been taught, and even experienced to a certain level.

Surely you have heard of the Pareto principle. That 80% of the results come from just 20% of the actions.

Let us now look into it deeper, and see how you can use it to create enormous wealth for yourself without spending a lot of time or even effort.

THE 80/20 LAWS YOU HAVE NEVER HEARD BEFORE

The Pareto Principle. It implies that 80% of your results come from 20% of your efforts.

I find it's true. And I find that it has enormous implications, reaching far beyond what is normally believed to be the practical implication of the rule.

Understood properly, this 80/20 principle can have enormous impact on your personal life as well as your business. I am not just talking about the bottomline, or the take home cashflow here. I am talking about the overall quality of your life.

Which is why understanding the deeper implications of the 80/20 rule will completely change the way you do things.

When I first heard about the Pareto principle, I

thought it is a neat way of managing time. And that it is. But that is just one tiny, unsophisticated, and low-impact use of the law.

In this section, I will outline some non-conventional ways in which the 80/20 rule can fundamentally alter the quality of your life, business and investment portfolio.

Nature is Ruthless

A vast majority of species that ever walked, swam, floated, flew or ran on this planet are now extinct. Entire species - extinct. The species that have survived are the ones best suited to this current environment.

A vast number of animals fall prey to higher predators. As you move up the food chain, the numbers shrink, but their likelihood of survival improves drastically.

In a free market, wealth gets concentrated into the hands of a select few, while others are left scrambling and gnawing over the leftovers.

This is how the natural order of things is. If it sounds cruel, then that is because it is cruel. I didn't make the laws. I don't even necessarily like it this way. But it is the way things are.

There is absolutely no equality or fairness in the nature.

And the same thing applies to the world of business, investment, politics, sports and relationships too. A vast majority of businesses will close shop before the tenth birthday. A vast majority of relationships that you have will either end badly, or fall by the wayside.

A significant majority of rising sportspersons, artists and politicians will amount to nothing over the long run, while a very small minority will rise to the top, and will go down the pages of history.

The 80/20 rule always works.

Try out a little experiment.

Go to forbes.com and pull up the list of ten wealthiest people on this planet. Then add up their net worth.

Next, add up the net worth of the wealthiest two people.

What you will find is that the wealthiest two or three control almost 80% of the total net worth of the top 10.

So even amongst the richest billionaires, the top 20% control 80% of the resources. That's how things are.

In any consolidated marketplace or industry, the two or three companies with the largest market shares have access to almost 85% of the market. All the other players all fight for the remaining 15%.

If you are a businessman or businesswoman, you could try out another little experiment. Pull up a list of all your clients and customers, and you will find that the top 20% bring in a vast majority of your revenues. In most cases, the top 20% of your clients bring in 80% of the revenues.

In fact, you could literally fire the bottom 10% or 20% of your clients or customers, and never miss them at all.

Why? Because they are bringing in less than 4% of your revenues in all likelihood.

Understand that a vast majority of things are bound to fail in life.

And while that sounds scary, if you would just alter your frame of view, it opens up a whole new world of possibilities for you that never existed before.

For the sake of brevity and simplicity, I have boiled the application of the 80/20 principle down to three laws. Three immutable laws that you must abide by, if you are to succeed.

Law 1: Prepare to Fail

Understand that most of your ventures are going to fail. Especially the untested ventures. An untested venture is one that is novel or new. Most such ventures are going to be utter disasters. Every once in a while, you must come across some ventures that almost succeed... these are the top 20%. For every hundred ventures you undertake, nearly eighty of those are bound to be a loss.

This is inevitable.

Another fifteen will be marginally profitable.

And four will be quite profitable.

Only one out of a hundred "ingenious" ideas you have will actually turn out to be ingenious in the real world.

If you understand this law fully, you not only save yourself a world of disappointment and fear, for you will be emotionally prepared to deal with a failure... you will also only risk that which you can afford to lose.

So many entrepreneurs put all their savings and capital into one big idea that they hope will be an immense success. Dazzled by the media that makes it appear that everyday a new Billionaire is born out of the spirit of entrepreneurialism.

While it might be true that the technological revolution has created far more multi millionaires, and billionaires than ever before... it is also true that an equally large army of ailing businesses and failing entrepreneurs go unnoticed and un-cited.

As a result, it is easy to be mislead into believing that success is right around the corner if you'd just be bold enough to take the leap.

Nothing could be further from the truth.

The reality is... that most every business you start will fail. No matter how good you are with management, marketing or operations.

The reality is that more than half your investments will underperform compared to the S&P 500.

And the reality is that woe is the fate of any investor or entrepreneur who invests more than he can afford to lose. I know, because I have been one of those starry eyed young entrepreneurs once. And I ended up not just broke, but over a quarter of a Million Dollars in debt.

At one point, I was indebted to literally every single

person who ever trusted me enough to lend me a dime or invest a dollar with me.

I have learned the hard way that things rarely go as planned. That most business plans crash and burn the minute you start advertising to the world.

I have learned the hard way that it takes 50 online advertising campaigns to find one that works profitably.

I have learned the hard way that it pays very well to be ready to fail. In fact, to expect failure, and to have the next thing lined up, so that you can move on immediately without wasting any time on mourning failure.

If most species of animals that roamed this planet have failed to survive, is it any wonder that an idea you thought would change the world actually fizzled?

Law 2: The world works the way it works, not the way you want it to work

I used to attend seminars related to investment, business growth, real estate, and wealth. And I'd be the easiest convert.

Not in terms of how easy it was to get me to sign up for one of these seminars, which it was. But in terms of how quickly I'd drink the kool-aid and believe each and every word the high maester, or the guru would utter.

I'd take their theory to be gospel, and I'd base my worldview on that. And I'd bet all my savings, again and again, on a feelgood theory that a supposedly "enlightened" guru proposed.

Things are different today.

Today, I do not trust any theory or philosophy easily. No matter who it comes from. No matter how successful they may seem or be. No matter how prudent and realistic they appear to be.

Today, I am only convinced by conducting a small test of my own.

Because a real test shows me how the world actually works, instead of how it ought to.

For instance, very recently, a friend of mine who I really trust told me about a new online advertising platform that is supposed to be a game changer. It's like an auction site for online advertising.

It is a very intriguing concept.

My friend claimed that it had been a game changer for quite a few people he knows. And that they had been getting over 300% returns on their advertising investments in terms of sales.

In theory it all made perfect sense.

However, I am no longer the same wet behind the ears kid I used to be many years ago. For me to base my advertising campaigns on any theory would require actual field testing of that theory.

Here's what I did...

I called up the company that runs this new advertising platform, and found that they required a minimum deposit of five hundred dollars. This would give me a sort of pre-paid advertising credit on their platform. I also found out that in case I wanted a refund, I could claim a refund of the unspent advertising credits, but there would be a 15% charge.

Since the concept made perfect sense to me in theory, I immediately deposited $500 to the platform, and spent $100 on advertising. The ads that I used were the ones that performed best for me on other platforms.

After spending $100 in advertising credits, not only did I not receive a single sale, but I also did not receive a single lead. That's correct.

On my other, supposedly expensive platforms, I continuously generate leads at $10 a piece. But on this "inexpensive" platform, I failed to generate a single lead for $100... despite using my best ads.

So I asked for a refund on the remaining $400, and got back $340 (they deducted a $60 restocking fee).

For the total cost of $160, I was able to invalidate the efficacy of a new advertising platform, at least for my current business.

I did not break bank. $160 is not a significant sum.

And this is just one example.

I constantly test new advertising platforms and avenues for as little money as I can. Sometimes I can perform a test for as little as $50. Other times, I end up paying $1000 for a test. Usually, I know in advance how much I stand to lose. In this case, I knew that if I could generate at least 5 leads for $100 spent, then I would bother with the platform. Anything less than that, and I'd be asking for a refund. I knew the maximum amount of money I could lose was $160, and that's all I lost.

And yet, every single day I see hopeful entrepreneurs deposit $3000, $5000, even $10,000 right from the start at the same platform. In many cases, this is their entire marketing budget.

I find it highly amusing, yet sad.

Just because someone you trust told you something does not mean that they can't be wrong.

Your best bet is to test everything for yourself.

Law #3: Allocate your resources disproportionately

We have established that the 80/20 rule is effective in most all situations in life.

In business, you often hear about the average cost of acquiring a client. About the average amount of revenue per transaction. About the average amount of profit per transaction. About the average amount of money spent on following up with existing clients. So on and so forth.

And yet, these statistics are meaningless, in terms of valuable business data.

If you have ten different advertisements, two of those are guaranteed to outperform the other eight put together.

If you have ten clients, the bulk of your profits are

guaranteed to come from just two clients.

Does it not then make perfect sense to allocate a higher proportion of your follow-up budget to these two best clients?

So many times I see businesses treating all their clients the exact same way. That is a colossal folly.

Your top 20% clients deserve the lion's share of your attention, as well as your resources. For they bring in the bulk of your profits.

Your top 20% advertisements deserve to be shown to 80% or more of your audience. For they drive the largest portion of sales.

Devote your attention and resources equally, and you have a formula for mediocrity.

Devote your a lion's share of your attention and resources to the best performing ads, the best stocks in your investment portfolio, the best clients you have, the best relationships you have in life, and the best activities that produce the results you desire... and you accelerate your profitability curve, as well as maximize the overall happiness in your life.

For instance, there are hundreds of ways of being healthy.

But if you were to just focus your attention to the following three tenets, and ignore everything else, you'll still be light years ahead of the vast majority of the population of this planet.

1. Watch what you eat. Eat meats and raw veggies for most of your calories, fruits, dairy, fats and nuts sparingly, and avoid drinking, smoking, and eating junk food.

2. Work out regularly. Lift heavy weights three times a week, and run for 30-60 seconds as fast as you can once a week. Keep your body active most of the day.

3. Sleep well. At least 6-8 hours each night. Do not compromise on your sleep.

Follow just these three tenets, and you'll be light years ahead of almost everybody you meet everyday.

In business, focus most of your attention and resources on your best clients, and you have a winning formula.

In my own business, at any time I will have one primary client (who I call partner), five secondary clients (who I call masterminds) and twenty five tertiary clients (who I call brainstorms).

I work on my partner's business with my own hands. As such the primary client's business gets 3 whole work days each week.

I talk to secondary clients (masterminds) for an hour once a week.

I meet with tertiary clients (brainstorms) once every three months.

Other than these, I only meet with the remaining

people once a year, at the annual convention. Of course, due to time limitations I am unable to devote significant amount of time to any of the clients present at the annual convention.

This arrangement where almost all my time is focused on the main client's business is proving to be very fruitful for me. Since I own equity in my main client's business, focusing almost half my working time on their business makes it possible for me to maximize my own wealth.

In business too, all activities are not created equal. I have found that best use of my time is spent working on the business, not in it.

As such, I always strive to break down my tasks into simpler mini-tasks that others can do, and into systems that anyone can run. Consequently, I end up having the time to focus on activities that bring in the maximum amount of money.

This law of disproportionate division of assets goes well beyond business and investment.

In your own personal life, you'd be well advised to spend most of your leisure time with your inner circle of family and friends, only spending a small amount of time with distant relatives, acquaintances, and business "friends".

Even in dating, I have found the 80/20 law to be very useful.

I found myself interested in only one girl out of the five girls who would indicate (indirectly) their interest in me. Then, of five girls who interested me, I'd only find myself compatible with one. And of five girls who both interested me, and were compatible with me, only one would really have common beliefs and values.

Of course, in personal life emotions get involved, and so with friends and family it is not always possible to practice 80/20.

But at least in business and investing, one must strive to.

Now, if you combine Law #2 (test everything), and Law #3 (allocate your resources disproportionately), it stands to reason that it would be in your best interest to invest a small amount of money into every single opportunity that comes your way.

Just be careful about two things...

1. Always start by investing as little as possible.

2. Never invest more than you can lose.

Sometimes, even the minimum commitment required to test out a new business idea, or a new investment opportunity is too large. In such cases, wait for the next opportunity or idea.

Just because everyone else tells you that something will work does not mean it will. Case in point: Bernie Madoff. Madoff made off with many Millions of Dollars that came from many smart investors who invested just because they saw others investing with him.

Crowds are easily led astray by con men. In fact, pretty much all conmen and scammers prefer to deal with crowds instead of dealing with people one-on-one.

So always test small. And test for yourself. If something works, great. Slowly increase your investment. If not, immediately withdraw.

Now, upon testing a hundred new ideas or ventures, you'll end up losing money in eighty. That is fine. Law #1 explicitly tells you to expect failure most of the time. And not be surprised by it, like most people are. Get rid of these immediately, and salvage all you can as soon as you humanly can.

Another fifteen will be marginal. You'd be wise to remove your involvement in these when you come across better opportunities.

Another four will be profitable. You should constantly be on the lookout for these, as these will make up a significant portion of your net worth, or investment portfolio.

And there will be on home run. The one big score. The one millionaire maker.

This idea or investment deserves as much of your capital as you can possibly invest.

However, Law#3 also states that your attention should be divided disproportionately. So don't spend too much time analyzing the $2000 stock investment, when you have a $50,000 investment in a new tech startup. That is what deserves a much larger portion of your attention.

MONEY
MANAGEMENT

TAKING CONTROL OF
PERSONAL FINANCES

You can earn a Million Dollars a month, and still be poor.

We have all heard of the poor guy or gal who won Millions in the lottery, and four years later ended up poorer than he or she was before winning the lottery.

We all have also heard, on the other hand, of the many men and women who have enriched their lives immensely, built up great fortunes, secured their family's financial position, as well as enjoyed a life full of richness, despite having a small start and without employing any unethical or illegal means to get ahead.

What's the difference?

The difference is in the management of money.

In the first section, we discussed how currency is only

symbolic, and about how inflation works. Yet, currency is, and will continue to be, the very best fluid conductor of wealth as there can be.

It does not matter how much you earn as long as your spending patterns do not support wealth building. Wealth is not built just by earning more. Wealth is amassed by spending what you earn judiciously.

A Tale Of Two Men

Imagine two young men, Rich and Drake. Imagine that money is like live butterflies. Both of them want to have a lot of butterflies.

Drake is a hard working man. He is also very smart. He knows that he isn't going to catch any butterflies sitting at home. So he goes into the nearest garden, and uses his net to catch a few butterflies. He spends all day working hard chasing the butterflies, and ends up catching a dozen. He then brings these butterflies home, and sets them free. Then he goes to sleep.

When he wakes up, he notices that some butterflies have died, while others have escaped. The only living butterfly is close to death.

So he goes to the garden again, and the entire sequence repeats itself.

One day, he explains his plight to a man who says to him, "If you want more butterflies, you should use a larger net. Even if some escape or die, you will still have more butterflies that live on."

This immediately resonates with Drake, so he spends valuable cash to buy a larger net from the salesman.

Lo and behold, his investment pays off. He is able to catch more butterflies with greater ease. And upon returning home, he sets them free and goes to sleep. When he wakes up, however, things are just as dismal as ever. Six butterflies are still alive, but barely. One seems to be healthy. Others have either escaped or died.

And the same cycle repeats itself. While the number of live butterflies in his house increases somewhat, he still is unable to find a way out. He still has to go out every single day to catch more butterflies.

Sure, if he does not go out one day, his home won't be empty. But if he doesn't go out for a few days, his home will eventually be empty.

He upgrades to a larger net as soon as he can afford to, but there is no escape.

On the other hand, Rich is adopting a different strategy.

From the very first day, Rich never bothered himself with buying a net to catch butterflies. Rich instead devoted his resources - his time, his attention, and his money to cultivating his own garden right outside his home.

He spends time, money and energy everyday to plant new trees and to take care of the tiny plants that shoot through the soil to take form.

He spends money to fertilize his little garden and to

ensure its safety from pests and weed.

He spends time to landscape his little garden.

In a few months, there is an abundance of flowers in his courtyard. These flowers naturally attract butterflies. He doesn't have to go out to chase the butterflies, the butterflies start coming to his garden.

As time passes, Rich invests more and more of his resources to increase the size of his garden.

Consequently, as his beautiful garden gets larger, the number of butterflies that enhance the beauty of the garden keeps increasing.

Rich never goes out to chase a single butterfly. Eventually, when there are enough butterflies in his garden, Rich says to himself, "Hmm. Now I can afford to slow down. In fact, I can choose not to work ever again. But since I like working on my garden, I'll continue doing it after I return from a one year vacation. In the meanwhile, I'll have a caretaker look after the garden."

While Drake will never be free of having to go out and catch butterflies, Rich already is.

The End.

Now, that is a metaphorical story. If you'd just replace the butterflies with incoming dollars, and garden with assets, you'd end up with the following story.

A Tale Of Two Men

Imagine two young men, Rich and Drake. Both of

them want to have a lot of income.

Drake is a hard workingman. He is also very smart. He knows that he isn't going to get any income sitting at home. So he goes into the nearest office, and uses his skills to get a job that given him a few dollars. He spends all day working hard chasing the dollars, and ends up making a few. He then brings these dollars home, and starts using them. Then he pays no attention to those dollars.

When the month ends, he notices that a portion of his income has been spent on his necessities, while the remaining income he somehow managed to waste. He's left with a hundred dollars, but he's got a couple of bills to take care of.

So he goes to the office and gets another salary, and the entire sequence repeats itself.

One day, he explains his plight to a man who says to him, "If you want more income, you should use a larger degree. Even if you waste some money, or live luxuriously, you will still save some money."

This immediately resonates with Drake, so he spends valuable cash and years to acquire a business degree from a reputed college.

Lo and behold, his investment pays off. He is able to get a bigger income with greater ease. And upon returning home, he spends freely without paying attention. When the month is up, however, things are just as dismal as ever. He has $700, but he's got a few bills to pay, and taxes are already overdue. It looks like he'll end up saving $200 though.

And the same cycle repeats itself. While his income and savings increase somewhat, he still is unable to find a way out of the rat race. He still has to go out every single day to work a job.

Sure, if he does not go for a day, or even a takes a whole moth off, his bank balance won't be empty. But if stops going altogether, in a few months, his balance will eventually be empty.

He gets promoted to a higher rank soon, but there is no escape, for his expenses increase proportionately.

On the other hand, Rich is adopting a different strategy.

Rich got himself a job. While he kept his expenses as low as he could, from the very first day, Rich never bothered himself with saving money. Rich instead devoted his resources - his spare time, his attention, and his surplus cash to cultivating his own assets.

He spent time, money and energy everyday to test new business ideas and to take care of the ones that proved profitable.

He spent money and used debt to buy tiny apartments that he would rent out for a tiny income.

He spent time to sell underperforming assets and to devote more resources to assets that performed well.

In a few years, he has a significant investment portfolio. These assets bring him cashflow every month. He doesn't have to go out to chase cashflow, the cash just flows into his account every month.

As time passes, Rich invests more and more of his resources to increase the size of his portfolio.

Consequently, as his well planned portfolio gets larger, the returns keep increasing.

Rich never goes out to chase income. Eventually, when he has more income coming from his investments than from his job, Rich says to himself, "Hmm. Now I can afford to quit my job. In fact, I can choose not to work ever again. But since I like working, I'll continue doing it after I return from a one year vacation. In the meanwhile, I'll keep an eye on my portfolio, and spend an hour every day just making sure that the assets continue performing well."

While Drake will never be free of his job, Rich already is.

The End.

The difference between Rich and Drake is not about how much they earn. In fact, Drake earns more than Rich does from the day job itself.

But Rich knows how to invest his spare income. He kept his expenses small and spent only what he needed to. He then invested the rest of his cash in acquiring assets that produced additional cashflow for him.

Eventually, he had enough assets in his portfolio that his income from the day-job was dwarfed by the cashflow from his assets.

That is when he realized he was financially free.

Defining Financial Freedom

When you have enough assets in your investment portfolio that you can not only live comfortably from the returns, but also reinvest a portion of your income from the assets to buy even more assets, you are financially free.

Let's say you and your family spend $75,000 a year to live comfortably, take a trip, pay your bills, and pay for your kids tuition.

Let's say you have $100,000 in your investment portfolio that bring in $18,000 a year in returns.

Are you financially free?

Of course not. You can't quit your job, or else you won't survive. At least not at the same standard of living.

But what if you had $1,000,000 worth of assets in your portfolio that gave you $180,000 a year. Now, even if you spent $75,000... you'd be able to reinvest $105,000 into your portfolio to buy more assets. That would increase your cashflow next year even more.

This becomes a self fulfilling prophecy. You can quit your job now, and still continue getting richer. Despite the inflation.

So let's say that inflation of goods and services is set at an average of 6% per year. That means your expenses will increase by 6% each year. And that your investment portfolio brings in a 18% return in terms of cashflow, so your $1,000,000 portfolio brings in $180,000.

Let's also assume that you reinvest your surplus cash at the same rate of return, and continue doing it for 20 years.

Here's how it will turn out...

In your twentieth year, your portfolio will be worth $10.596 Million. Your income will be over $1.9 Million, while your expenses would have risen to $227,000. You'll have over $1.68 Million to reinvest at the end of the year.

As you can see, once your portfolio brings in more money than you need, your net worth keeps increasing even if you don't make any more money from your day job.

This is financial freedom.

And this is what you should be heading towards.

As soon as you are financially free, you can retire form your day job. You'll still continue getting "richer".

Now understand that you don't necessarily have to quit. If you like what you are doing, you are certainly welcome to continue doing it. You'll get wealthy that much faster.

Financial Freedom is important because from it stems the time freedom. Time freedom is basically having control over your time. You get to decide what you want to do and when.

You also get location freedom. You are free to be wherever you want to be on the planet after you have the financial freedom. You can travel the world, and still continue getting richer.

And here's the one thing that financial freedom depends upon...

How You Spend Your Money

I can make ten times more money than you, but if you spend your money wisely, while I spend it foolishly, then you are bound to end up wealthier than me.

The remainder of this section is a discussion of how to spend your money. A reminder - This section is about personal finance only.

But the principles of personal finance can be applied with equally powerful results to any financial entity. Be it a corporation, a household, a fund, even a city or a country. The same principles can be applied.

As usual, I have found that while there are many things one can do to enhance one's net worth, there are only two laws that if one pays attention to, he or she may be completely free of all others.

Law #1: Separate income into different bank accounts as soon as you receive it.

I have four different bank accounts. All four are personal.

My first account is for saving. At this time, I save 5% of my income. I will stop saving in a few months, though. Why? Because this account will end up having enough money to cover all my expenses for two years.

My bank pays out 9% return on a fixed deposit. Since I am never going to withdraw this money, unless I face a dire emergency, I'll end up beating inflation on my savings. Not by a huge margin, but sufficient to make me feel comfortable.

I can access this money in a matter of seconds if I need to. All I will forgo is the interest earned that year.

The second bank account I have is for investments. At present, I devote 50% of my income to investment. As soon as I make money, even if it's just $5000, I take $2500 out and put them into this account. As soon as the next investment opportunity presents itself, I invest money from this account.

I have a diversified, yet focused investment portfolio, and it's getting better. Since I am going to devote two whole sections to investment, I'm not discussing my investment strategy here.

The third account I have is for expenses. Currently valued at 40% of my income. This means, I can not spend more than 40% of my income.

When I was just getting started and my income was very low, I used to spend as much as 80%. Even though my expenses were low, my income was too low, and so I had to spend most of what I made to survive. As my financial position improved, the percentage of my income I require for maintaining a much more comfortable lifestyle has declined.

Eventually, this will go down to 10%. I imagine this will happen not spontaneously, but over the course of the next decade.

The remaining 5% get deposited into the fourth account. I cannot reveal what I do with this money, but it's a kind of miscellaneous expense.

Now, for you, I recommend getting at least three accounts. One saving, and two current.

The saving account is for your savings, of course.

The two current accounts are for your expenses, and for your investments.

This is the bare minimum.

If you have a regular expense of some other kind, for instance a hobby, perhaps, or a charity that you like to contribute to, then get a fourth current account too.

Now, as soon as you get any income - be it your salary, or a return on one of your investments... divide that income up into your accounts.

This way you maintain complete control of your financial future.

Of course, there is no way for me to tell you what percentage of your income should you spend... it depends upon a lot of factors. But generally speaking, if your income is low, and if you are just getting started, or have a family to support financially, then you'd devote a large portion of your income to expenses, and reserve a minor portion of saving and for investments.

On the other hand, if you have a nice income, keeping your expenses low would be a wise strategy.

A friend of mine who works at an investment-banking firm makes upwards of $200,000 a year in salary after paying taxes, yet his monthly expenses are less than $2000. I find that smart. Just 12% of his income is spent on living. He doesn't save anymore, for he already has over $250,000 in savings. Should he lose his job, he'll be able to live on his savings account for ten years.

And his investment portfolio is worth $1,000,000. Last year, his return from his investments exceeded $120,000.

He is financially free. While he can quit his job at any time, he continues to work, and invest almost 88% of his income into buying up assets.

I wouldn't be surprised if he ends up making, just from his investments over $1,000,000 a year within the next decade.

So pick a strategy for yourself right now.

Decide what portion of your income you are going to spend, and what you are going to invest, and how much you will save.

Generally speaking, you want to save at least six months worth of expenses as soon as you can.

Once you have saved enough to cover your expenses for six months, then it's prudent to start investing.

I personally feel very secure once I have at least two years worth of expenses in my savings account.

While your strategy is your own to decide, I highly recommend separating bank accounts for your expenses, savings and investments.

I also propose you make it a law to divide all your income into your bank accounts according to your strategy as soon as you receive it.

Law #2 Buy Only What's Necessary

Groceries & Bills should form the bulk of your expenses. If you are spending a lot of money on buying things that you don't really need, or don't regularly use, then that's a waste of money.

It goes without saying that touching your saving or investment accounts to buy "stuff" is an absolutely cardinal sin.

But even if you are spending money from your expense account to buy things that you don't need, then that's frivolity. This frivolity costs you in terms of how much longer it will take you to become financially free.

The less you waste, the faster you become financially free.

I personally don't like to buy anything I won't use at least once a week. And I hate buying things that distract me or waste my time.

For instance, for the last ten years, I have not had a TV. Never had one, never missed it, never used it. An average American spends over 14 hours a week on TV. Over the last decade, I have not only saved myself 7,280 hours of mind numbing spectatorship, I have also managed to read well over 350 books in this time.

Time well spent, I'd say.

Of course it has also saved me at least $20,000 in inflation adjusted dollars I'd have spent on buying TV sets and paying for the cable, and then impulsively buying more products upon seeing advertisements and infomercials in the TV over the last ten years.

I have used a simple formula to enhance my wardrobe as well.

I found that I'd get most compliments about my appearance, and most shy glances from girls when I put on a dark colored suit with a white shirt.

So I decided to redesign my wardrobe.

Five white shirts, three suits, two pairs of leather shoes and matching belts, 20 ties and as many pocket squares, a dozen cuff links and tie-clips, and two overcoats. Apart from that, I have two pairs of jeans, one jacket, and one sweater. Seven pairs of black socks and underwear. That's it.

Every time I wear something out, I just replace it. You will never find me randomly shopping for apparel. I get custom tailored suits and shirts only, and those last me a very long time.

Almost no impulse purchases there, apart from a couple of T-shirts every year here and there.

I recently compared my wardrobe expenses with my brother. Over the last four years I spent $2100 each year on the wardrobe. He spent nearly $1600 last year.

Here's the difference - My suits cost $2000 at least. He's got a $400 off-the-shelf suit. I get compliments all the time on my dressing sense. I have never heard him get one. All my clothes are custom tailored. All his clothes are either too tight, or too loose.

And most importantly, I have someone pickup my laundry every fifteen days, and do it for me. He does his laundry himself.

I also make a lot more money than him, because he's still a student and borrows money from home.

So knowing what you need, and then buying smartly actually saves you not only money, but time. And makes you look like a Million Dollars. Not a bad deal at all.

Over time I have gotten rid of a lot of things I bought needlessly. The more things I get rid of, the more I realize how little I truly need to be happy.

I find myself buying a new book every week, though. That's a $100 a month expense right there that most people don't have, but strangely enough, I find it a useful one.

You should not have any problem splurging for a high quality mattress, for instance. Because you are going to use it everyday, and the quality of mattress greatly affects the quality of your sleep. And the quality of your sleep greatly affects the quality of your life.

You should not have worry about spending money for good food or good clothes. So many times I see people spending $6 on an expensive coffee while bemoaning how they can't afford to buy fruit at Trader Joe's because it's

50% more expensive.

Everything we do is to live a good lifestyle. And a good lifestyle is about eating well, sleeping well, feeling powerful and secure, and doing things you like to do. You might enjoy spending time with your friends having a drink, and so accounting $150 a month for that into your expense account is not a bad idea. You might enjoy learning guitar so spending $200 a month for lessons and repairs is a good idea.

But buying things you really don't need - like ten different sunglasses, or five 40' TVs - is highly discourage able.

Just follow these two laws, and you are well on your way to financial freedom and enormous wealth.

Keep your expenses low, while maintaining a healthy and satisfying lifestyle, save enough to cover your expenses for six months, and invest all the rest.

I am a huge proponent of making success inevitable. These laws make it inevitable that your spending will be restricted to essentials only.

So chalk out your spending strategy right now.

And then let's move on to the investment strategy.

ASSETS

Before we determine a strategy for you to own assets, let us first understand what an asset is, and what a liability is. Investment is the process of using your capital resources to acquire assets.

When you use your money to buy, for instance, stock in a well run company, you have made an investment.

A stock in a well run company is an asset. But not all stocks are assets. Some stocks can be liabilities as well.

Let's start by defining an asset.

An asset is anything tangible or intangible that produces an income on a regular basis. Anything that produces a regular inflow of cash - be it monthly, weekly, or annually- is an asset.

Anything that costs money to maintain is a liability.

If you ask most people, they'd tell you that their greatest "asset" is their house. Which is a fallacy. See, a house that you're living in is not an asset, it's a liability.

Why?

Because it costs money to maintain. It costs money in repairs. It costs money to run in the form of bills.

If you own a house and live in it, you know that you are spending money on a regular basis to maintain that house.

And as such, a house that one resides in is a liability. Not an asset.

On the other hand, if you have a property that you own and rent out, it brings in a monthly inflow of cash. Sure you may spend a small portion of that income in maintaining that property, but largely, it brings in an inflow of cash.

Such a house is an asset.

So the next time you are confused about whether something is an asset or a liability, simply ask yourself if it costs you money to maintain. If it does, then it's a liability. If it makes money, then it's an asset.

The key to building wealth is owning as many assets as you can, and to minimize the liabilities that you have.

The more assets you have, the higher your cash inflow is. The more liabilities you have, the higher your cash outflow is.

We spoke about minimizing and managing your liabilities in the previous section. Now we are going to talk about maximizing your assets.

Financial freedom is the stage where your assets bring in more inflow of cash than your liabilities take out.

So if the sum total of your liabilities is $2000 a month, or $24,000 a year, but you own an apartment that brings in $3000 a month in rent, then you are financially free.

The process of acquiring assets is known as investment.

In this section, I'll talk about the different kinds of assets investors own, along with the merits and demerits of investing in each kind.

But before we examine the different kinds of assets, it is imperative to understand this...

Cash itself is not an asset. While a lot of companies will list cash on the asset column of their balance sheet, cash itself, from the point of view of an investor is not an asset.

You see, cash does not produce an income. If you place a $100 bill in someone's pocket, it doesn't magically become $110.

So, when you add money to your investment account, the purpose is to actually make an investment at some point of time. If possible, soon.

Your capital is not invested until you buy an asset.

Having said that, let's talk about the different kinds of assets.

Asset #1. Real Estate

Real Estate is an asset, if properly utilized. Most people buy a piece of property to either sell it a higher price, or to develop it somewhat and to then flip it at a higher price point.

When you buy a property for $100,000 and sell it for $130,00... then the $30,000 gain is known as a "Capital Gain."

While it's great to have capital gains upon selling an asset, your investment strategy should not rely upon a probably sale.

If you buy an asset thinking along the lines of "I will sell it for 30% more within X months" then you are speculating. Sure you may be able to sell. Sure you might even sell it at an even higher price point than your estimate. Sure you might even make a lot of money in capital gains.

But that purchase is not a wise investment.

A wise investment is about returns, not capital gains.

People who buy while predicting capital gains are speculators, not investors.

Investment is about returns, and purely returns. In a wise investment, it does not matter whether you ever sell or not, because a wise investment gives you an asset that produces a regular cashflow for you.

So if you buy something with a short term speculative capital gain in mind, you run the risk of never being able to sell it. You are highly likely not to be able to sell it for a while.

A good investment automatically brings you patience. Even if you never sell it, you are not too concerned. Because your investment continues to produce a desirable return regularly.

Nobody can predict how long it will take for an asset's value to go up. The value of an asset might even go down temporarily, or even for a longer period of time.

Therefore, you should never buy an asset based on an imaginary sale price. Always buy an asset based on how much cash inflow it produces.

And always make an investment as though you are investing forever, and you never intend to sell.

Like I said above, it's nice to have a capital gain. But you can never predict when your asset will sell, and how much it will sell for.

So your investment should be based on the cashflow alone.

What is a good Rate of Return?

I personally consider anything above 18% return a good rate of return. Anything above 20% is great, and anything above 25% is unbelievable. These numbers generally beat inflation in the modern times, though that isn't likely to be true for very long. But that's the subject matter that requires its own discussion, and is beyond the scope of the current discussion.

Obviously a "good" rate of return cannot be defined,

simply because all investment is inherently risky. The higher the rate of return, the more there is a risk of losing your invested capital.

While some investors might be risk-tolerant and desirous of a high rate of return, others might be risk-averse and simply like to beat inflation.

Everyone's investment strategy is different.

Nevertheless, the stock market averages around a 15% rate of return over the long term. So if you were to invest all your investment capital in S&P 500 Index funds, you'd be able to average a 15% return on your investment over the long term.

Since investing in the S&P 500 does not really require a great deal of research or analysis at all, if I am unable to produce at least 15% return on my own, I'd rather invest in S&P 500 blindly.

One can become very wealthy by simply investing in the S&P 500 funds.

But the objective of developing your own investment strategy is to consistently beat S&P 500 by a certain margin. This margin is why we invest time and effort in developing an investment strategy.

But if you do not have the time, or the inclination to put in the effort to develop your own investment strategy, investing in S&P 500 funds is a good idea, and is fairly simple and straightforward.

But stocks are not the only kinds of assets. If you

recall, we were talking about real estate.

When you buy real estate, examine it on the basis of the following two points.

1. Is the cash inflow from rent (after deducting average maintain and repair costs, as well as property taxes) a good enough return on your investment?
2. Will there be increasing demand for rental properties in that area over the next few years while you recover your investment?

The first point is a mere calculation.

Say a multi family home is available for $500,000. And that it has five units each renting out $2000 a month. The annual taxes and other liabilities amount to $30,000.

The gross cash inflow from rent is $120,000 a year. The outflow is $30,000. Therefore the net return is $90,000 a year.

That's an 18% return on the $500,000 investment.

If I continue to make 18% a year, there is no need for me to ever sell the property. Unless someone makes me a very lucrative offer, I might never sell it.

The second point, however, requires a little more research.

The basic idea behind supply and demand of real estate is this... Are new jobs being created in that area? If new jobs are being created in a city, or a nearby city that is less than one hour away, then it's safe to assume that rents will go up.

If the job market looks bleak, however, don't invest in that area.

These two points apply to pretty much all investments. Not just real estate investments.

When comparing investments, always invest in that which brings a higher return, and has the potential to bring in an even higher return in the near future, based on economic factors. In case of real estate, the economic factor that really matters is the local job market. People move wherever their jobs take them, and they need a place to stay.

Asset #2. Stock in Publicly Traded Companies

As I said above, S&P 500 is the place to start. The index averages 15% return on investors' capital over the long term, and that's a decent rate of return.

The good thing about stock market is that you can start small. Really small. If you are able to invest only $200 a month, there may not be a lot of real estate for you to buy. But nobody's stopping you from buying a couple of shares in any company you like.

Once again, the financial analysis is simple. Ask yourself if the cashflow from the stock is a good return for your investment. Shares of a company give out dividends. You can take any company and look at a history of share prices as well as dividends.

For example, let's take Coca Cola.

The share of the company traded at $12.72 in 1995,

and today it's worth $44.83. But if you bought one share in 1995, you'd have two shares today.

Why? Because in 2012, the company splintered its shares. Everyone who had one share got two, who had two shares go four, and so on. Doesn't change anything from our point of view.

Note: The capital gain averages out at 10.8% per year over the long term per year.

Now, I notice that they have issued four quarterly dividends this year, each valued at $0.305. The total money issued in dividends is $1.22 In other words, if I had a share, I'd get $1.22 in dividends this year.

Now, one year ago, each share of Coca Cola traded at $40.46 and had I bought one share then, I'd have made $1.22 in cashflow.

That's a 3.01% return in dividends.

With shares, simply add the return from dividends as well as capital gains.

So my $40.46 investment would have brought in $1.22 in cashflow, plus $4.37 in appreciation (capital gain). The total return would be $5.59, or 13.81%

That's one year analysis.

Now let's do a ten year analysis.

Ten years ago, one share of Coca Cola sold for $20.26. Over the last ten years, the total dividend each share has brought in amounts to $17.24, and I'd have two shares (instead of one) at $44.83.

So the total return on my $20.26 investment over the last ten years would be $17.24 from dividends, plus the capital gain. The current value of two shares is $89.66. So the total return is $86.64.

Averaged out, that is a 18.1% return on the investment.

I'm not surprised that this company is beating S&P 500. It's owned partly by Warren Buffet, the greatest investor this world has ever seen.

By the way, to download a rate of return calculator, simply go to www.LakshayBehl.com/Calculators and download a complimentary return calculator. Simply plug the investment amount, the appreciation, the cash inflow, and the number of years, and it will tell you the average rate of return.

To summarize, if you want to decide whether or not you should buy stock in an individual company, simply do a one year, a five year, and a ten year analysis.

If the company consistently returns more than 16% annually, then it's a very good company to invest in.

You can find all this information about any publicly traded company's dividends and price history on the internet.

Using this freely available information as well as our calculator, you can analyze any company and see if it's worth buying a share in.

This extremely simple approach focuses your attention on the numbers that truly matter to you as an investor. It ignores a large number of statistics that mean very little to an investor. For instance, ROE, ROA, Value of the Assets etc.

None of these statistics matter as much as historical return on share price, when you are buying a share in the company.

Of course, there are a variety of analysis approaches. But this approach, I've found, takes into account some of the very best.

The first person to influence Warren Buffet's philosophy is Benjamin Graham, who himself was a wealthy investor and ran a fund where Buffet was employed for the first few years of his career.

Graham's philosophy, outlined in his outstanding book, The Intelligent Investor is based on being able to buy undervalued securities.

In other words, if a security is worth $100, ad you are able to buy it at $85, then you ought to buy it, no matter what it is.

That's what Graham said, and that is what Buffet started out with as his core investment philosophy.

The method that I just outlined does just that - it enables us to price the value of a stock on the basis of our desired rate of return.

In the example of Coca Cola, had the share price risen

by the same $4.37 over the last year, and produced the same $1.22 in returns... and the only difference were that I'd have to buy it at $80 a piece to get the $5.59 in return, then I'd have a 6.99% return instead of 13.81%.

That means, I'd have bought an overvalued share.

If the return is high enough, then you have necessarily been able to buy the share cheaply.

In the stock market, it often makes sense to go against the grain. Most investors are largely emotionally driven speculators. As a result, they sell when the market is fearful, and the prices drop. That is when an Intelligent Investor ought to buy.

The same $5.59 return could have been a 16% return had I bought the share at $35, and the same $5.59 return could be a 12% return had I bought the share at $45.

When you think about the rate of return, you necessarily force yourself to buy cheap.

Often, you'll find your best bargain when everyone else is selling.

The upside to buying shares in a company is that the current and historical financial information for larger companies is largely easily available.

That, and that getting started requires a very small capital.

But the downside is that your dividends are typically low. A large portion of your return is built into the capital gain aspect. Since the current market price is always visible, this is not a hindrance. But you must realize that your cashflow is going to be significantly smaller than the actual return you see.

This is because these companies are valued at a very large multiple of their earnings. Publicly traded companies are valued at anywhere between fifteen and twenty-eight times their annual profits. And that produces a conspicuous downside for an investor.

If you plan to invest in the stock market over the long term, while on one hand the value of your portfolio will rapidly grow thanks to the appreciation of share prices, on the other hand the cash flow you receive will be dismally low.

This will inevitably delay your achievement of financial freedom.

Secondly, the number of years it takes you to break even purely from dividends is very high. If you do not sell your shares, expect to break even after as many as fifteen to twenty-five years.

Asset #3. Franchises

Owning a proven profitable franchise is a fantastic way of producing a return on your capital.

While there are many franchise options available, the solid, proven and risk-free franchise outlets are rather expensive to start.

However, due to a nationwide (or even global) marketing and advertising campaign typically run by the corporation selling the franchise, you don't really have to do anything.

Once a staff has been hired, it is basically a cash cow.

I plan to eventually own quite a few franchises.

Franchise income is relatively stable, the return is typically high, and requires very little work to run. The marketing and branding is pretty much always done for you, and all you do is sit back and collect.

However, there are downsides. Like I said, it's not possible to be a franchisor unless you have at least $200,000 to start with. This is the reason why I don't own many franchises yet. The initial investment is significant.

From the financial point of view, calculation is rather simple.

If you invest $200,000 and get to take home $60,000 a year, you make a 30% return.

Of course how much you make varies, but for the most part, franchises of successful companies like McDonald's and Starbucks are unlikely to produce very small returns for the investor - or else they would not have tens of thousands of investors in the first place.

They have proven sales systems in place, and so for an investor with a large enough portfolio, a franchise (or a few) is a must-have.

Asset #4. Gold, Precious Metals & Commodities

Since they do not produce any cashflow at all, and

produce only a capital gain, these aren't pure assets.

I like to think of gold as a device to store wealth. It's a saving device. If you want to save money for the long term, buying gold could be the way to do it. The thing about life is that it's short. *__And as such, wasting years of your life just storing wealth instead of investing seems like a waste.__*

The good thing about gold and some precious metals is that they often beat inflation easily. This is because the amount of gold available in the world is limited.

While we can print as many currency bills as we want, we can't magically conjure up more gold.

So as we print up more and more bills, the price of each ounce of gold keeps rising proportionately.

Consequently, if you invest in gold, or commodities, you are hedged against the inflation. But there won't be any cashflow whatsoever.

Asset #5. Angel Investing

Now this is for investors who have a portfolio of several million dollars. In 2015 dollars, I'd say $3,000,000 or more only.

You can choose to invest in startups in exchange for equity in the company.

This is a very high risk and very high return investment avenue, and not for the faint of heart.

But for the sake of completion, I find it convenient to

mention it among the various categories of investments.

If you are going to invest in new technologies, or new companies, be prepared to lose your capital in almost 80% of the companies. 80% of the companies will not survive, and you will lose a large portion of your capital invested in these companies.

Another 15% will survive, and you will end up making a decent return here. Say 15% to 40%.

4% will be profitable and you'll see an extremely good rate of return on these companies. Somewhere between 40% and 60%.

1% of the companies will take you by surprise, take the world by a storm, and literally cover for all your losses, and more. These breakout companies are what you are looking for. In such companies a small $100,000 investment easily nets over $10,000,000 or more. And rapidly.

Like I said, angel investing is suitable for only those who have at least $3,000,000 or more in capital available. Even then you will find yourself partnering up with other investors like yourself to create an investment fund.

Even the 1% breakouts are not guaranteed. It all comes down to your ability to spot talent and predict trends.

If you back companies with solid products that actually have a chance to get adopted by the world, and if you consistently back teams of proven experts, then you're doing well. Even then, don't expect more than one company in 25 to do well, and more than one in a hundred to breakout.

This is a dangerous game. But one breakout company can be a game changer for you.

You can literally catapult your $10 Million portfolio into a $100 Million fortune with just one right investment.

And yet to find that right investment you might have to weed through fifty, eighty, even one hundred poor and average ones.

Asset #6. Your Own Successful Business

This is the best asset of them all.

Why?

Two reasons. First - because by and large, you control the fate of your company.

If your company is making $200,000 a year in cashflow and you don't find a way to take it to $2,000,000 a year, then blame lies with you.

Sure, market factors affect businesses. Sure as the economy goes up or down, your company will go up or down.

But for the most part, it is up to you (or your team) to make a company grow faster than its competitors, gain market share, exponentially increase profitability, and expand.

People are never going to stop buying. If they stop buying from you, then it's up to you to make a fresh offer to them that they find seductive and tempting.

Real Estate depends largely upon the job market of the local region.

Stock market is invariably out of your control.

Prices of gold and commodities are not yours to control either.

Franchises work on their own, and there is not much you can go accelerate their growth, or to salvage them from auto-destruction.

Startups are inherently volatile and there is little you can do to control them.

But your own businesses, well, you can and you do control them.

For the most part, Warren Buffet himself likes to own a majority of shares in the companies that he invests in. So that he becomes a managing partner. This gives him control to do pretty much any thing he wants to do.

He can choose a new CEO, or replace the entire management if he so desires. He can affect strategy, and build Joint Ventures with other companies if he deems them profitable.

Since you control the fate your own business, your own business then becomes a very lucrative kind of asset. And that's the first reason why I love it.

The second reason is profitability.

While the companies listed on the stock market are grossly overpriced in relation to their earnings, companies you privately own are not.

When you buy a profitable company, you can expect as much as 15% to 30% return in cash from the very first year.

I am looking at a company that is for sale right now because the owner wants to retire after having run the business for more than four decades. He wants $6.5 Million for his company that produces $1.5 Million in annual cashflow.

That's a 23% rate of return. It would take less than five years for the investor to break even.

It's a stable company with a staff of 19 people, that includes a fully autonomous management staff of four.

Certainly then, even if you don't intend to control such a company, it'd be very wise to invest in one as a sleeping partner, just for the return.

As such, small and medium sized companies that are priced between five and ten times their annual cashflow are an ideal asset.

The returns are high, the cashflow dividend is high, and the potential for growth is high.

The downside is that it takes a large capital to own a company like this. This downside is overcome by the means of Private Equity funds.

Private Equity funds are funds created by pooling together capital from anywhere between three and fifty private investors.

All investors invest a significant amount of money to pool together enough money to buy out a company.

Still, to participate in a private equity fund, you typically need at least $100,000 to $500,000 to invest.

While this business model is inaccessible to most all investors who do not have a large enough portfolio to warrant such an investment, we have made it possible to invest a fraction of that amount, and be a sleeping partner in a profitable and well established small business that we manage.

For more details, visit www.BehlCap.com

And that covers all the main kinds of assets you can own as an investor. Clearly all have their pros and cons. We will discuss the ideal investment strategy in the next section.

What is important is that you start investing as soon as you possibly can, and that you invest on the basis of returns.

If you achieve a reasonable return with a particular asset, then invest. Otherwise, don't.

The reason why I ask you to put away a certain percentage of all your income in a separate bank account is so that when an investment opportunity presents itself, you know where to look for capital.

Now let's talk about investment strategy.

DIVERSIFY

There are two schools of thought.

The first one says don't put all your eggs in one basket.

The second one says identify the one (or a very small number of) baskets that are safe and produce a reasonable return, and then invest all your eggs in those baskets.

Which one is right? Which one is wrong?

I agree with both.

Allow me to explain.

See, when someone talks about diversification of investment portfolio, a real estate investor thinks about buying more properties in more geographic areas. A securities investor thinks about diversifying his capital in different companies. A private equity investor thinks diversifying means buying up many different small companies instead of one medium sized company.

Yet this is not what I mean by diversification at all.

To me a diversified investment portfolio looks something like this...

While there is a huge variation in the cashflow produced by the various kinds of assets, as well as their appreciation, a well diversified portfolio contains them all.

While the highest amount of investment has been made to PE fund and Angel fund because they produce the highest return rate, a smart investor hedges himself against the risk by diversifying into all kinds of assets.

And that is truly the essence of hedging. Diversify yourself so that if depression hits, and the stock market as well as hedge funds fail to produce adequate returns for a couple of years, other markets that are relatively unaffected continue to perform well.

Overall, a well diversified portfolio produces a reasonable rate of return, even during distressing times.

Your own personal investment strategy varies with your income, and available capital for investment.

If you only have a few hundred, or a few thousand dollars in investment capital, then your options are limited to either stock markets or stock markets.

There really isn't much else that you can invest in at all.

But as your portfolio grows, and you start making cashflow from your investments, and your available capital goes into tens of thousands of dollars, you can start investing in gold funds and hedge funds.

While gold produces no cashflow, so I'd recommend against investing in gold right off the bat... hedge funds do produce a better cashflow than the stock market.

Then in a few years, when you have enough capital that ranges into hundreds of thousands of dollars, invest in real estate, PE funds, and buy franchises.

This really accelerates the growth rate of your portfolio, since real estate, PE funds and franchises produce a very high cashflow.

Finally, when you have capital available in Millions, jump into angel funds.

These jumps are not made daily. When you jump from a few hundred dollars to tens of thousands of dollars, your portfolio is already worth a few hundred thousand dollars by that time.

This takes at least 5-7 years to build.

When you jump from hedge funds into real estate, it takes another 5-7 years to make that jump.

Overall, all four jumps require between sixteen and thirty years. To build up a portfolio like the one I listed above takes an entire career. But then, it produces over two Million Dollars a year in cashflow. In addition to that, it appreciates by over Two Million Dollars a year on its own.

As you continue investing and reinvesting, the numbers go up exponentially.

As you can see, you can't be expected to diversify right away. Simply because with just a few thousand dollars in available capital, you can't be a part of PE funds, or Angel funds, or even hedge funds.

Nevertheless, investment is a way of life for serious investors. Even if you make only $1000 a month and invest only $200 a month - you are still light years ahead of the vast majority of the population who do not care to invest at all.

If you are wondering whether you should save first or invest first, I suggest you do both. In what proportion you save and invest is up to you. But generally, I recommend putting away no less than 10% of your income into the investment account, and at least 5% of your income into the saving account.

Once you have enough saving and have stopped saving, it's advisable to put away at least 15% of your income into your investment account.

Even if your income is low, and your expenses eat up most of what you make, you must have the financial discipline and will power to put away at least 15%. Preferably more.

As usual, your own investment strategy varies greatly depending upon your income, your obligations and liabilities, your risk-aversion, your ambition, so on and so forth.

In my monthly newsletter, I discuss an intelligent investor's investment strategy each month. Many investors have told me that just the investment strategy contained in the newsletter is far more valuable than the price of the newsletter.

It is accessible at www.LakshayBehl.com/NewsLetter

You can get your first issue for free using the coupon code "201456wealth".

FOCUS – THE ULTIMATE INVESTMENT STRATEGY

In the previous section we examined how a well diversified investment portfolio is all about branching out into various kids of assets.

In this section, we re going to focus in greater detail upon how to choose, for instance, a stock to buy from the thousands available. Or a company to acquire as a PE firm from the tens of thousands available.

If you take the S&P 500, and do a ten year analysis on all the companies therein, you will find that almost 400 are below average performers (returning less than 15% return) while another 75 are average producers (returning slightly over 15%).

Then there are twenty that really outperform the S&P 500 by a significant margin (returning between 18% and 25%)

And finally here are five that grossly outperform the index by a huge margin producing 25% or higher returns.

The easiest thing to do in the world for a smart investor, then, would be to buy the shares of one of these five companies.

Of course there are day to day fluctuations based on the emotions of fear and greed that drive the average investor, and two or three of these high performing stocks will be overpriced, while the other two will be underpriced.

It makes sense to pick the ones that are underpriced.

We evaluated in some detail in the section on 80/20 principles the need to disproportionally allocate your resources. Well, this is it.

If I had only $1000 to invest, I'd buy $800 worth of stock from the top two best performing companies, while the remaining $200 I'd invest in the next three best performing companies.

Stock market investments produce returns in two ways - Capital gains (which means appreciation in the value of the stock) and cashflow (in the form of dividend) from the market.

In the beginning, I'd be biased towards stocks that pay out a greater proportion of the return in terms of cashflow (or dividends) as opposed to capital gain (in the form of appreciation).

Their historical performance is an indication of how they pay out.

Let us compare two different companies.

Coca Cola has, over the last ten years, paid out $17.24 in cash dividends on a share that could be bought for $20.26, and the current value of that one share is roughly $88.

Using the growth calculator found at www.LakshayBehl.com/Calculators you can see that the rate of return in terms of cash flow is 6.4%, while in terms of capital gain it is 15.8%.

Now let's look at Microsoft.

The share traded at $26.60 ten years ago. Today it trades at $48.42.

The share produced $6.26 in dividends over the last ten years.

Rate of return in terms of cashflow is 2.14%. Rate of return in terms of capital gain is 6.2%.

Clearly, investment in Coca Cola seems to be the better choice. The overall rate of return is high, the rate of return in terms of cashflow is also higher, and the rate of return in terms of capital gain is also higher for Coca Cola.

Now, these numbers look very small, and they indeed are. Many an investor gets discouraged at the sight of such small numbers, hoping to produce miraculous returns in a short period of time.

But here's something I'd like you to consider...

If you only started out with a $2500 a month salary,

and invested only 20% of your income at 18%, and got a 5% increment in salary each year, and reinvested all your dividends... at the end of your career of forty years you'll have amassed a fortune worth over $34 Million Dollars.

Now that's not a small number at all.

I'd like to paraphrase Bill Gates who said most people overestimate what they can do in one year, but grossly underestimate what they can do over a decade.

In investments, the longer you invest, the sweeter the fruit.

Of course, as your portfolio diversifies, you will end up making a higher return on your overall portfolio too.

Moving On...

The point of this section is for you to understand that not all investments are created equal.

There are stocks that produce four and five times as much return as another stock.

There are franchises that produce 30% return, and there are those that produce a paltry 4% return.

Your resources are best invested disproportionately.

Look at the history of performance of any investment. Understand that if it does not have a history of performance, it's a highly risky investment and it's highly likely to fail. Part performance is the barometer with which you estimate future performance.

Instead of buying 30 different stocks, I recommend

you focus on a maximum of four to five stocks at a time. This gives you time to focus not just on the financial aspect of the investment, but also on the factors that ensure a superior performance over the upcoming years.

Factors such as the skill of the management team that's running the company. Such as the reputation of the products, the services, and the customer support of that company. Factors such as how easy or difficult it is for a competitor to enter the marketplace, and how high the barrier to entry is.

One must buy each share of a company as though he is buying the entire company itself. How much due diligence would you do if you were buying a whole company?

That is the kind of due diligence you need to perform when you buy a single share in a company.

Here are some of the things you would look at...

1. The value of the assets that the company owns. Assets could by anything. Real estate, furniture, furnishings, equipment, inventory etc.

2. The cashflow of the company. The EBITDA. This is the net profit a company makes.

3. The amount of debt and other liabilities that the company owes.

4. The experience and effectiveness of the management team that's running the company.

5. The value of the brand.

6. The reputation of the company's products and services among clients and customers

7. And finally the historic rates of return

Now of course this is a time and labor intensive process. Which is why the strategy of focusing on just five companies that grossly outperform the S&P index makes perfect sense. You can devote a few hours to five companies before deciding how much you'll invest and where.

You can not do that, obviously, if you are considering fifty companies, or worse 500.

Most investors unfortunately buy and sell stock based on the emotions of fear and greed. This is rather illogical, as they end up buying when the morale is high, the markets are up, and the prices are high, and selling when the market is fearful, and the prices are low. They don't take the time to study the company carefully enough before investing.

While we are talking about stock exchanges, I want to make it clear that there are two kinds of people who buy and sell shares. Investors and speculators.

Investors perform what is known as fundamental trading. Speculators perform what is known as technical trading.

Whereas investors focus on the fundamentals, and invest for the long term, preferring to buy a quality stock at reasonable prices, speculators try to make money from the day-to-day fluctuations in stock prices.

It should be noted that speculation is a zero some game. For some speculators to make money, others necessarily have to lose. The reason for this is simple. No value is created in just buying and selling of stock.

For value to be created, the company actually has to produce and sell a product or service using the funds accumulated from selling stock.

I recommend you completely forget about the intraday speculative technical trading, and focus completely on fundamental investing, wherein you invest for the long haul.

Onwards...

Now, as you can reasonably understand, when such detailed analysis is required even to buy a small stock holding in a company, a more detailed analysis is required when you move up to the other more sophisticated and larger kinds of investments.

When investing in real estate, here are the questions you need to be asking yourself...

1. Are there new jobs being created nearby? Why or why not?

2. What is the current market price?

3. What is the current rental rate?

4. Is the property overpriced or underpriced?

5. How much money will be spent on the maintenance and repairs of the property upon the completion of sale.

6. And how much will be spent yearly? What about property taxes?

7. Does this financial investment produce a decent return in terms of rental cashflow?

Generally, if you can't obtain even 12% of the purchase price through rentals, the property is overpriced. If you can obtain more than 15% return through rentals, the property is reasonably priced.

Keep in mind that you are never to speculate on how much it will sell for five or ten years down the line. Your property deal has to be profitable right off the bat, based on the rental income.

While angel investing is largely speculative in nature, investing with a fund that has a track record of investing in fast-growing startups helps.

But most importantly, you don't want to hold five different real estate assets. Instead, focus on buying one large asset.

You don't want to hold stock in thirty different companies, you want to hold more stock in three or four well-performing companies.

You don't want to invest in five different hedge funds, you invest in one.

You don't invest in four private equity funds, you invest in one.

Intensity beats extensiveness every time.

Focusing on a few gives you the power to focus on your investments deeply and observe them regularly. While most people who invest for the long term like to invest and forget about their investments, we recommend paying at least a few hours of attention each year to each of your investments.

That's the first reason why you need to focus on a few investments of each kind.

The second reason is that there are many opportunities out there, but there only a few really good opportunities that come your way. By saying NO to the bad and mediocre opportunities, you keep your attention, and your resources free for the good ones. Even Warren Buffet and Charlie Munger, the full time Multi-Billionaire Investors hold a rather limited number of investments. This because they like to pay attention to all their investments on a very regular basis. As a result, they have managed to outperform the S&P index by almost 25% on an average over the last 40 years.

Now that's a track record worth writing home about.

NET PRESENT VALUE

When the financial analysis boils down to a single question - whether or not to invest in an opportunity, it finally comes down to financial analysis.

The most important question you must ask yourself is how long will it take you to recover your investment, at the present value of it.

So here are two immutable laws of finance:

1. The value of $100 today is more than that of $100 a year from now. The value of $100 a year from now is more than that of $100 two years from now.

2. The value of $100 a year ago was more than it is today. The value of $100 two years ago was more than it was one year ago.

It is simple. If I asked you to give me $100 today, and

in exchange I were to promise to give you $100 back five years from now, would you do a deal with me? Of course not.

The reasons are obvious. The further away in the future I promise to return it, the more interest you would want. This is because the likelihood of your investment yielding a fruit diminishes as time goes on. Anything that can go wrong will go wrong. Future is unclear and the risks involved increase as more time passes. This uncertainty and risk has to be accounted for in terms of a reasonable rate of interest.

The second reason why is because there is inflation. You simply would not be able to buy as many goods and services for $100 five years in the future as you can buy today.

The third reason is that there is an opportunity cost. You have a limited amount of capital. If you can invest it in a place where it could yield a 17% return for you, why would you lend it to me for a lesser return?

Mathematically, this concept can explained through the concept of Net Present Value.

Simply put, the present value of money can be calculated using the following formula.

Present Value = Future Value / ((1 + Expected Return Rate)^ Number of Years)

For example, if you expect to make a 20% return on your investment, and someone promises you $1,000,000 at the end of five years, then simply calculate the present value of those one Million Dollars.

Present Value = $1,000,000 / ((1+20%)^5) = $401,877

In other words you should invest no more than $401,877 today if you wish to achieve a 20% rate of return, and the only payment you will get is $1,000,000 at the end of five years.

But what if you were to receive multiple payments at multiple time intervals? How do you make your analysis then?

So let's say I propose to you that I'll give you $200,000 each year for five years starting from the end of this year. Let's assume you want to achieve a 20% Rate of Return.

All you need to do is download the net Present Value Calculator from www.LakshayBehl.com/Calculators and enter the values as follows.

Notice how the net present value is $598,123. Compare this to the previous example where I offered you a lump-sum of $1,000,000 at the end of five years. The present value of that was only $401,877.

Further notice how the present value of $200,000 keeps falling the further away into the future you go.

In most investment opportunities that you will come across other than stock market, the question you will need to ask yourself is how much is this worth to me.

And the answer, based on finance, should be straightforward.

Step #1. Determine how much return you want on your investment.

Step #2. Determine how long you are willing to wait in order to break even.

Step #3. Predict the future cashflows from that investment.

Step #4. Calculate the present value of those future values.

Step #5. Add those present values, and find the Net Present Value.

This net present value or NPV is what you should pay at most for the opportunity.

Let's take a concrete example.

A company I might end up buying is on sale for a certain amount. It produced One Million Five Hundred Thousand Dollars last year in cashflow, or EBITDA (Earnings before Interest, Taxes, Depreciation and Amortization).

I also know that its cashflow increases by 10% annually, but for the sake of being conservative, I am going to ignore that fact, and assume that it will continue to produce $1.5 Million each year.

How much should I be willing to pay to buy this company?

Let's follow the steps.

Step #1. How much return do you want?

Since I can easily get 15% from S&P 500, I like to achieve 20% return on such a large investment that requires so much time and effort.

Step #2. How long are you willing to wait to break even.

The company will continue to produce cashflow for me as long as I continue to own it, but I like to break even within five years.

Step #3. Predict future cashflows.

I have already assumed that cashflow for the next five years is going to be $1.5 Million.

Step #4. Calculate present values.

Using the NPV calculator, I find the present values...

Step #5. Calculate NPV

Adding all present values, I see the NPV is $4,486,000. In other words, I should pay no more than roughly $4.5 Million for this company. The present owner of this company, however, wants $6.5 Million. Unless he agrees to sell for $4.5 Million or less, this deal won't go through.

Now, this is just an illustrative example. But it perfectly illustrates how easy it is for you to determine whether or not an investment opportunity is right for you.

While things are straightforward in the stock market - there are clear dividends and clear stock values, things are often unclear in all the other investment opportunities.

The Net Present Value method is your perfect ally

when it comes to deftly navigating the treacherous waters of high finance.

Base your calculations on it, and you won't be lead astray, so long as your projects are conservative, and valid.

This is especially useful for real estate deals. With real estate deals, however, I am perfectly happy getting a 12% return, and breaking even in 15 years. Why? Because I can easily get bankers to finance a large portion of those deals at 6%.

So calculate the Net Present Value based on conservative estimates of the future cashflows, and you will know which opportunity is underpriced, and which one is overpriced.

BUSINESS
OWNERSHIP

OLD IS GOLD

While it is well known that owning a business of your own is the easiest and fastest way of growing your net worth rapidly, increasing your own income exponentially, and laying down a solid foundation for a secure financial future for yourself and your family, often times people think that the only way to do this is by starting your own company, and painstakingly taking it through the various stages of growth.

Nothing could be further from the truth.

If you are an entrepreneur with an idea and a few thousand dollars in your pocket, by all means go ahead and start a company. But know this and prepare for his beforehand - that your company is more likely to fail than it is to succeed.

We studied this while we studied the 80/20 principle. Most new companies fail. Most new business ideas never germinate. Most "visions" of the future that entrepreneurs get riled up over never amount to a single sale.

If I had $2000, I'd rather invest them with Coca Cola instead of starting my own business. Why? Because $2000 gives me just one shot at making some sales. Chances are, I am wrong. Chances are that the market will not get as excited about my product as I predict.

Very often I see entrepreneurs starting up companies with their money, only to end up crestfallen and disappointed at the end of the day that their business did not take off like they had hoped.

Very early on in life I learned that the world works the way it works not the way I want it to work.

The odds of a new business surviving three years are less than 20%. For online businesses the odds are less than 4%. Those numbers are dismal.

Benjamin Graham had two rules for investment. Rule Number 1 was "Don't Lose Your Capital." Rule Number 2 was "Don't Forget Rule Number 1."

If you lose half your capital, you'd have to make a 100% return just to bounce back. What are the odds of that happening? Virtually zero.

Therefore, a prudent investor does not invest in high risk ventures until his or her financial future is extremely secure.

Will I ever invest in high tech companies, new technologies, revolutionary new products? Of course. I might actually get involved with, or even start such companies at some point of time.

But that will only be when my family's financial future is extremely secure. When my investments are bringing in cashflow that amounts to at least three times my family's expenses for living a comfortable life. Then I'll experiment with new technologies and revolutionary new ideas.

And even then, I'll invest my time, money, energy and attention with full awareness that the odds are still going to be against me.

I am good at business growth. Give me a company that's making $1,000,000 a year, and I will take it to $2,000,000 a year within twelve months, and to $10,000,000 within three years. I am good like that. I understand how business systems work, and I know how to build powerful sales systems that obliterate competition.

And yet, I can not guarantee that a new business idea will survive.

Richard Koch, the multi Billionaire co-owner of Koch industries, and the author of "The 80/20 Principle" says in his landmark book that business ideas are the DNA of a business. Whether or not that DNA is suitable to survive in the current atmosphere can not be predicted.

My business growth skills are similar to healthy lifestyle choices. For any person with the DNA that's able to survive in this ecosphere, I can put them on a nutrition, sleep and exercise program and vastly enhance their health. But I can not help them if their DNA cannot survive in the modern ecosystem.

Similarly I can help businesses that have ideas (their business DNA) that survive in the current economy. This can only be known through sales. If their products and services sell at a reasonable profit, then the idea behind the company is sound. And I can, through business systems and sales systems greatly enhance the profitability of such a company.

But if the DNA is flawed, if the company is based on an idea that customers do not pull out their wallets for, then there is nothing that I can do. Nor can the greatest business consultant in the world.

As such, for the time being, until my own financial future is secure, I would prefer to steer clear of investing in, or getting involved with companies that have unproven, untested DNA. I'd rather take a mildly profitable company and grow it. Because a mildly profitable company that has lasted ten years despite of virtually invisible sales systems, and chaotic business process management has already proven that its DNA is viable. That the idea behind the company is sound, and that people are buying what it produces.

I can work with that.

But with an untested idea, a revolutionary new technology, a game-changer kind of thing, you never know if it will work. You might think it's the greatest thing since sliced bread, but nobody else might buy your product or service.

My recommendation to every business owner and

entrepreneur is to hold their horses until their financial future is secure.

Do not dabble in the unknown, for pioneers often wind up dead along the sides of a road never before travelled with arrows in their backs. Unless you can afford to lose $20,000 on a new idea, and then immediately move on to invest another $20,000 in another new venture, and continue doing so until you find a winning DNA, my suggestion would be to invest safe.

New businesses, new ideas, new companies in emerging new industries are untested and unproven. As such any capital devoted to these is not investment, but speculation.

As a rule of thumb, you should not be playing a game of speculation with more than 3% of your capital at any time. In other words, unless your investment portfolio is at least $3,000,000 or larger, you shouldn't be investing in new ideas, new startups, new technologies, new industries, new companies etc.

Sure every now and then a game changer comes along that literally catapults an investor's portfolio from eight figures to nine within a matter of months. But for every success story the media glorifies, there are a thousand failures that lie in the wake of the same promise of riches. You never hear about those, but they are out there. So many people lose their shirts over new ideas. Yet it is so much better to just invest in a proven company.

If you are interested in owning, managing and growing

a small business, my suggestion is buy a company that produces at least $200,000 a year in profits. These companies are known as micro-caps. And there is an enormous amount of companies like this that the owners want to retire from, especially now. There are not as many buyers as there are sellers, so the prices are very low. Most such companies end up never selling at all, and the owners just close shop salvaging what they can by selling their assets for dirt cheap prices.

My suggestion would be to buy such a company and then use your entrepreneurial chops to grow it from $200,000 a year to $2,000,000 a year, and then use that immense cashflow to build a solid portfolio of stocks, hedge funds, gold funds, franchises and real estate. Within a few years your portfolio can amount to over $10,000,000 and produce upwards of $1,000,000 a year in cashflow itself.

Only then should you start testing the unproven NEW ideas.

Of course, not everyone wants to own, manage, run and grow a business. You may not have the time, the inclination, or the motivation to do so.

If that applies to you, then invest in one of the other assets we discussed in the previous sections. Alternatively, if you are interested in being a sleeping partner while reaping the high returns of micro-caps, invest with a private equity fund.

If you do not have a few hundred thousand dollars

that it takes to participate in a private equity fund, then visit www.BehlCap.com. This is my private equity fund, and the minimum amount of capital required to participate makes it easy for anyone to jump in.

We follow the philosophy of investing only in proven companies. In addition to being profitable, these companies must also be well established and have a well trained staff, as well as a layer of management at least. This ensures smooth transition. At Behl Capital, we focus on just one company at a time. We buy just one company and then focus on growing it as big as we can. Before we move on to the next company, we completely maximize the profitability of our previous acquisition, and completely systemize it.

All the principles of investment and financial planning that you have learned so far, and those that you are about to discover in the upcoming sections are put to practical use with all our acquisitions.

The reason why I am telling you all this is because I want you to know that I practice what I preach. In fact, I have been practicing it for quite a while now, whereas I am only preaching it for the first time in this program. So all the principles you are learning are sound, proven, and actually deliver results in the real world.

Like I said before, I do not trust anybody's word. I like to test every theory, every philosophy, and every law out for myself. Consequently, everything you are reading in this program is field tested. I have personally tested it to ensure the efficacy of this financial philosophy.

So if you are a budding entrepreneur getting ready to spend thousands of dollars on an untested idea, know that the odds of success are against you, and that the most practical thing to do right now would be to build up your capital into a large portfolio over the next few years by investing in proven companies, whether small or large.

Buy assets. Not possibilities.

FIVE TRAITS OF A HIGHLY SUCCESSFUL BUSINESS

Whether you are investing in stocks, or you are buying a company yourself, or you're investing in a Private Equity fund, you need to pay attention not only to the quantitative aspect of the business that we have already discussed in the previous sections, but also the qualitative aspect.

This section deals with the five traits of a highly successful business. Any business with a proven DNA, and the following seven traits is inevitably going to succeed, and grow.

While two different companies might appear to be exactly the same upon rigorous financial analysis, upon careful examination, one business often trumps other in terms of these qualitative traits.

While the financial analysis allows you to predict the

future financial performance based on past performance, the qualitative analysis that we are about to discuss actually enables the longevity of a company.

The following five traits are common to virtually any company on track to a long and prosperous future in the economic marketplace. You can observe most, if not all of the following traits in any successful and rapidly growing company. Without further ado, let us examine these five traits.

Trait # 1. Fiercely Guarded Reputation

Any company that takes is reputation lightly is a company that won't survive very long in the marketplace, for a competitor who cares about his reputation is going to show up on the scene sooner or later, and obliterate this company by carefully cultivating and zealously guarding its own reputation.

Reputation is everything.

It's why people pay five times more for a commodity. It's why customers feel the pride of ownership of a product or service. It's why clients become fans and zealously and passionately argue with people who insult a brand.

If the company you are investing in does not care much about its reputation, then you would do well to look for another company to invest in.

Most businesses end up acquiring reputations that the owners and managers find undesirable. This is because they never actually sat down and took the time to decide what their company would be known for. Since they do not carefully cultivate or engineer a reputation, it's no wonder that the only thing to be said about their reputation is that "It Varies."

Furthermore, if by their sheer hard work and dedication they somehow manage to acquire a positive reputation instead of a neutral or negative one, they do nothing to guard it. Anyone and everyone can easily besmirch it, and they would have no way to guard against it.

Successful companies always start by carefully engineering a reputation of their own choice for their company. Then they zealously guard that reputation, taking extreme steps to overshadow any falterings and misgivings.

Avis' famous "We Try Harder" is not just an advertising campaign or a company slogan, it's their reputation. It's the guiding principle behind almost all their company policies. And they zealously guard this reputation by going the extra mile every time. Anytime an employee fails to go the extra mile for the client, heads roll. People get fired. They are that zealous about protecting their reputation. And the consequence is visible.

Trait # 2. Solid Sales System

Powerful companies have sales systems.

They know for every $10,000 spent in advertising, they are going to get $100,000 in sales. So on and so forth. Their marketing and sales systems are predictable and reliable. Their offers are lucrative and draw their audience in like moths to a flame.

Furthermore, they have multiple high end premium

offers for their elite clientele. Not everyone who buys coffee at Starbucks buys their $3000 coffee machine, but enough people do to warrant giving those machines shelf space.

When McDonald's went to India, they faced a peculiar challenge. Since it was the first multi-national food chain to ever set foot in India, most Indian people believed it would be expensive. Even though McDonald's has always had a reputation for being quite cheap in the United States, in India, they found themselves in this unintended predicament.

Luckily, they always think in terms of sales systems.

So they decided to offer a fourteen cent ice cream cone. That's right. An ice cream cone for mere fourteen cents. This was cheap, even from the Indian standards.

Just as soon as they started advertising the cheap ice creams, a crowd of people emerged at the various McDonald's outlets in the Indian cities. Once people were there, many of them paid more money than they were used to paying for burgers, just because they were there. McDonald's knew that as long as they could bring people in, they'd be able to sell their other products as well. And so they decided to lose money on those ice cream cones to attract crowds. And the strategy worked. Today there are thousands of successful McDonald's outlets in India.

A sales system that attracts crowds and then converts them into buyers of higher priced products seamlessly is guaranteed to topple competitors and create a powerful presence in the marketplace.

Trait #3. Process Systemization

There are two kinds of companies.

In the first kind, whenever a stapler is lost, Suzie needs to spend fifteen minutes looking for it, and the entire back office is disturbed to the point of being rattled.

In the second kind, everything is systemized. From the correct amount of ingredients to be used in a product, to the temperature at which it is to be cooked, and the number of seconds it takes, to which person is responsible for which stage of production and delivery, everything is a flawless system.

My thoughts run back to extremely well run companies such as McDonald's, Subway, and Domino's Pizza. There are hundreds of burger joints I have eaten at that I find sell a much better burger than McDonald's. There are numerous pizza joints that sell way more delicious and scrumptious pizzas than Domino's. And yet, none of these companies with seemingly better products have nearly as much market share as these behemoths.

Why?

In one word - Systems.

Not only do these large companies have powerful sales systems to bring in customers, and move products, but they also have equally powerful operational systems on the backend enabling these companies to serve their customers just as rapidly as the orders come in.

These systems are largely unbreakable, and the staff members are virtually fungible. You could take anyone, let them go through the training, and have them working their role in the system within a matter of days.

If every single process requires managerial approval before being deployed, the company is in a bad situation. If on the other hand, a company can run almost without any managerial interference, then you have a fully systemized money making machine that can outgrow any competitor as well as any geographic boundary.

I personally just focus most of my attention on sales systems and business systems when I take on a primary client. Engineering a reputation is a one time job that requires occasional revisiting. But development of systems enables any company to grow at an unprecedented rate of growth, which is what I like to see.

It's easy to sell franchises to a fully systemized business. It's easy to branch out. It's easy to sell such a company, because the new owner wouldn't have to do anything other than collecting his dividends every year.

Systems are the engines that drive a company's growth. Therefore they require dedicated focus from whoever is running the company. Be it you, your partner, a CEO, or whoever.

Trait # 4. Clear Hierarchy & Decision Making Powers

If a board needs to approve every move the CEO makes, then the CEO doesn't really have any power. And as such, he or she ought not to be held responsible for any results or lack thereof.

If one person has two bosses that they theoretically report to, then actually they report to no one at all. Everyone should know exactly who they report to.

If people don't have clear job titles with more importantly clear job description, then don't be surprised when they don't do what they need to do. Their job responsibilities need to be made very clear from the day they are hired.

Whatever gets inspected, gets respected. You should trust your staff, but still verify everything yourself. A good friend of mine has a company that sells real estate investment opportunities. To find prospects, he had hired a team of ten outbound cold callers. These people were supposed to dial 200 phone numbers every day, and locate the five or ten prospects who were interested.

Since this friend of mine as extremely busy, he paid virtually no attention to his telecalling department. Nor did he appoint anyone to hold the callers accountable. As a consequence, I personally found out that between the ten of them, they were making less than 400 calls a day, and generating ten leads in all, when they could have been generating fifty.

Here's the funny thing - My friend brought me in as a consultant to help them improve their conversions, because they had told him repeatedly that the reason why they weren't producing more leads was either because they didn't have enough training, or because they did not have a powerful enough sales script.

Of course I trained them, and rebuilt a new sales script for them, but not before appointing someone strictly to hold them accountable for making 200 calls a day. Within three days, the team was producing over sixty leads each day.

By the time I was done, they were producing more than one hundred leads every single day. My friend was incredulous. He could not believe that the same sales staff could produce 900% more leads.

I wanted to go further with it and fire some of the less productive members, and hire new blood, but my friend did not like that idea, and remained satisfied with the same results.

In actuality, the top three callers were getting over 85 leads. While the remaining seven would manage the other ten to fifteen leads. I was determined to fire the other seven and hire new blood to find winners, but my friend did not let me.

80/20 always works. Whether it works in your favor or against you is up to you.

The funny thing was, upon careful inspection I found that even before I had stepped in, the same people who were now the top producers were producing almost all the ten leads everyday, with the exception of one lead coming from someone else every other day.

My friend could simply have fired those seven people

even without hiring me, and his calling department's efficiency would have shot up by 300%.

Nevertheless the key in this case was to appoint someone they all reported to, who ensured that they were doing what they were hired to do instead of sitting idly and gossiping about how difficult it was to find interested prospects.

One last thing. If a company describes a process in such a manner as, "Well, Lucy here writes the newsletter. Then Dave prints out as many copies as we need and then Ramsey delivers it to the post office" instead of "Our marketing manager writes the newsletter, while the logistics in-charge prints out as many copies as needed, and then has the logistics assistant deliver those to the post office. The entire operation is overseen by the marketing manager, Lucy" then you know that they don't have a clear organizational structure.

Many newly formed companies like to operate with open door policies and without formal organizational structures. None of these companies ever succeed in the long run. Eventually, either a smart CEO changes these policies to ensure the company's survival, or these companies cease to exist.

A formal, yet ever-evolving organizational structure is key to any company's success.

Trait # 5. Constant Innovation

If a company constantly comes out with new products, services, offers and campaigns, and avoids frivolous waste on untested campaigns, then that company is suited for growth.

Let's face it - marketplaces are constantly evolving. New products cannibalize old products all the time. New technologies obliterate older technologies, and new companies eat up the marketshare of old companies.

Evolution and change continue to occur. The only thing that differs is whether a company makes its own products obsolete, or lets someone else do it for them, and take their marketshare as a result.

Constantly innovating is what keeps a company fresh. It gives them a reason to follow up with their prospects and clients. It forces them to be on a lookout for new technologies and trends. It forces them to think about what their clients innate wants are before the clients have verbalized those demands.

Apple is famous for innovating new products that constantly cannibalize their own existing products. Yet, with each new iteration, they evolve, and stay light years ahead of all competitors.

Innovation is not just technical, though it can surely be technology driven. Sometimes, innovation is simply found in presenting the same products and services in a different light. At other times, innovation is found in adopting new channels of marketing that while other industries have repeatedly used, this industry hasn't.

For instance, most industries have found it immensely profitable to advertise on TV, and use celebrity endorsements. Yet a vast majority of newsletter publishers have stupidly and stubbornly refused to use celebrities and advertise on TV. It'd be nothing less than marketing innovation for a newsletter publisher to flirt with the use of celebrity endorsement and TV advertising.

You would be best suited to invest in companies that have all, or at least four of these five traits. For such companies are virtually guaranteed longevity in the marketplace.

STRONG EXIT

In this section we discuss the various reasons why an intelligent investor might find it prudent to exit an investment by selling an asset. After discussing the reasons why an exit might make sense, we will discuss the right price to sell, and the right time to sell an asset.

Just as your own personal fortune depends largely upon how well you spend your income, and not just on how much you earn, your net worth depends largely upon how strongly you exit an investment, and not just how well you invested, and how prudently you acquired the said asset.

Let us start with a discussion of reasons.

A private equity fund might sell a profitable business they own to a larger fund or a publicly traded company after having maximized its profitability and after having built out its systems to as much efficiency as possible. Similarly an entrepreneur or a business owner who owns a successful established company might want to sell it. The reason why they'd sell it is primarily because it is taking too much of their time, attention and energy to own this company. The secondary reason why they'd sell it is to gain a windfall of capital gain, which they can then use to buy some other asset of their choice.

Private Equity firms usually buy and sell companies profitably and then go on to buy the next company which they'll sell in a few years. That's how they maximize their shareholder's wealth.

Business owners typically sell when they are ready to retire, or to move on to another phase in their lives. A successful business sale frees up capital so that they may acquire a larger, more desirable asset of their choice.

You might want to sell off your shares in a publicly traded company once you have built up a large enough portfolio when you see a profitable real estate deal present itself.

Retirement is another reason why a lot of people sell some or all of their assets. They might want to enjoy the finest luxuries that life has to offer, or they might want to pass down the capital to the next generation, or they might want to donate some of their capital gains to charity.

There are many reasons to sell your assets.

But for an intelligent investor, there is just one. **The capital acquired from the sale of an asset can be used to acquire a larger, or a more desirable asset.**

If you can sell $100,000 worth of stocks that produce 16%, and then invest in a P/E fund that can potentially produce upwards of 25%, then it would be very prudent to sell your stock and invest in the Private Equity fund.

In this section, we will see what to sell, in what order to sell your assets, what to sell them for, and when to sell them.

Let's start with the what.

What To Sell

The first asset you should sell is the least performing one. If you own shares in three companies that produce a total rate of return as 14%, 17.5% and 19% respectively, then it makes perfect sense to sell the shares that produce 14% first, as soon as you have an opportunity to buy an asset that outperforms it.

The next thing to sell would be the stock that produces 17.5% investment.

Let's say you have $200,000 invested in each of these shares. Let's say that now you have an opportunity to buy into a private equity deal and the buy-in is $300,000. This private equity deal is poised to make you 20%.

Then you'd sell $200,000 worth of stock that produces 14% and then $100,000 worth of stock that produces 17.5%.

You still retain $100,000 worth of the 17.5% yielding stock, and $200,000 worth of stock that produces 19%. Why? Because you don't have a better opportunity right now.

In this particular case, it would also be prudent to invest the minimum amount of money in the private equity fund. While you can easily sell all $600,000 worth of shares and invest your entire capital in the private equity fund, that move would not be advisable.

Why?

Because you want to diversify your investment portfolio across kinds of assets. If your entire capital is invested in one kind of assets, you are not immune to the fluctuations of that particular market.

So, you sell $300,000 worth of your lowest performing shares, and invest half of your capital in private equity, while retaining the other half in the admittedly lower performing stock market.

Recall the perfectly diversified investment portfolio we saw in the section titled "Diversify". Even though some kinds of assets produce a larger return than others, we still want to diversify our portfolio by investing in as many different kinds of assets as we possibly can.

So that answers what to sell, and in what order.

Now, let's talk about what to sell them for.

How Much To Sell Them For

In the case of publicly traded stock, you really don't have much control over the price. But incase of other assets, there might be room for negotiation.

For instance, I might be selling a piece of property, and there is definitely room for negotiation there. I might be selling a privately owned company, and there's a lot of room for negotiation there.

In such cases, obviously it makes sense to get as much as you can for your assets. But with any negotiation, when you are selling, the key is to know your absolute lower limit. The number below which you will not accept the deal. The lowest price you will accept for your asset.

So let's take an example.

Say you have a property that brings in, after deducting the liabilities, a sum of $25,000 a year. Now you are contemplating selling it, so that you may invest in a private equity deal that is poised to bring a cashflow return of 12.5%.

To make $25,000 a year from the private equity deal, at a return rate of 12.5%, I'd need to invest at least $200,000 in the private equity deal.

But I like to take a 20% margin of safety in such situations. So in this case, I'd sell the property for $240,000, and invest $240,000 in the private equity deal. I wouldn't mind if the supply and demand economics bring me a higher amount. But I wouldn't sell the property for less than $240,000. Even if it means not being able to buy in on the private equity deal.

My margin of safety is 20%. You might feel comfortable with 10%, or you may need 35%. That is for you to decide. When I move my own capital from one kind of assets to another, I need at least a 20% margin of safety. If I can't get a 20% margin of safety, the deal doesn't really make sense to me.

With that said, let's recap on when to sell an asset.

For a prudent investor, investment is for life. A prudent investor doesn't wait for a capital gains to live a good quality life, he depends upon the cashflow instead. So your mindset with exiting a kind of asset shouldn't be about getting a windfall and then spending that money on living luxuriously.

Your guiding philosophy behind exiting investments should be about moving assets from one kind to another, or diversifying, or even cutting down on the risk you might be exposed to.

So for instance, sometimes, you'll sell a business you own that produced a 30% return, and instead buy 3 franchises that produce 20%, and invest the remaining capital in the S&P 500 at 15%. Why would you accept a lower return? Because now your capital is diversified making you less exposed to fluctuations in one industry, and secondly you've freed up your time too simultaneously.

Nevertheless, the point remains. Any savvy investor never spends his or her capital or the capital gain received. He only spends a portion of the cashflow to buy whatever he needs to buy, while reinvesting the remainder to grow his portfolio.

Remember the first rule of investment. "Don't lose the capital".

LAWS OF THE GAME

THE IMMUTABLE MAXIMS OF THE GAME OF WEALTH

Wealth acquisition is a game. Nothing more, nothing less. There are laws that govern the game play, and then there are rules and winning strategies to abode by for those who wish to succeed in this game.

In this section, I am going to summarize the maxims and laws of wealth acquisition.

Maxim #1. Money is, and has never been, anything more than a symbol for wealth. Money is simply a tool that lubricates commerce.

Money is a tool.

Like any tool, you can use it either for creation or for destruction of your own health, wealth and relationships.

Money itself is not an asset. But a prudent investor

always uses as much of his money to acquire assets as he can.

Maxim #2. We are wired to spend immediately, and we are biologically programmed to seek instant gratification.

It takes careful cultivation of will power, and an acute awareness of the game to see how bad our own financial habits are. Often we end up spending money on things we do not need, and don't even want.

If you spend money buying things that you do not need, then sooner or later you'll end up selling things you do need. I think Warren Buffet said this first.

It is our biological drive to consume as soon as possible. To seek instant gratification of the body, mind and senses. We have very little control over what we buy, and what spend out money on. A significant portion of most people's incomes are spent on impulse purchases. Things they don't even need.

Cultivate willpower to curb your baser instincts.

Maxim 3. People with strong boundaries are not easily stressed. Even when they are, they beat anger with assertiveness, and anxiety with proactive action.

Savvy investors never make any big decisions when they are hungry, angry, lonely, or tired. It is imperative to be rational and cool when making financial decisions, and really any decisions that you make.

The first thing to understand is that there are things

that are within your control, and then there are things outside of your control. Having a thorough understanding of what lies within and without the realm of your control is what is known as having strong boundaries. What other people think, say or do is outside your control, and hence any attempt to change, alter or control it inevitably fruitless, and bound to create frustration for you.

So long as you focus on your own boundaries and only on what resides inside your control, you gain respect from others, and avoid mental turmoil.

Now, despite having strong boundaries, you might feel angry at times when you feel hurt by someone else's words or actions. In such cases, it is wise to be assertive with them, and to channel your anger into getting your needs met.

Similarly, when you feel anxious, it is best to channel that nervousness and take positive action. So for instance, if you are feeling anxious about your financial situation, working on a plan to make extra money, or adjusting your investment portfolio will not only alleviate your anxiety, but also make you feel more confident.

Maxim #4. The more (perceived) value you provide, the higher you can charge for it.

It is very easy to sell something for $10 when the buyer perceives it to be worth $100 to him or her. Easy flow of currency and goods is facilitated through differentials in value.

Value is largely based on perception. There is no

inherent value in sitting in a glass box with some celebrities and watching a game live. Yet people routinely pay hundreds of thousands of dollars for such an experience.

Value is also based on demand and supply. If you are the only seller of water in a desert, you can charge whatever you want, and you will find takers. Water in a desert is valuable. Very valuable. It's life giving. And therefore people will hand over their entire fortunes to you in exchange for a gallon of water.

Maxim #5. We all have a natural resistance towards someone taking a higher proportion of profits than us. This is known as the psychological justice mechanism. Subdue your own justice mechanism, and a plethora of deals will open up for you.

Nobody wants to make $25 when his or her partner makes $75. However, if you subdue this part of your brain, and train yourself to see multiple opportunities, there will be no dearth of financial deals available for you to pick and choose from.

The key to earning a lot of money is leverage. This leverage comes from other people's resources. Their contacts, their reputation, their assets are all leverageable.

If you can find a plan to leverage their resources, and make them an additional $100,000... And if you are willing to do all the work while letting them keep 75% of the profits, and taking only 25% of the profits for yourself, then you can access all their resources as much as you want.

Understand that you wouldn't make those $25,000 had

it not been for their resources. It is better to make $25,000 on a $100,000 deal than $20,000 from a $30,000 deal.

Someone who you make $75,000 will welcome you with open arms every time you want to leverage their resources. Someone who made only $10,000 while you made $20,000 will invariably resent you, and resist every idea you have thereafter. That's their own psychological justice mechanism playing up.

Maxim #5. There is abundance of everything you want in life, and everything you can dream of. There is abundance of wealth out there for you to take.

All it takes is boldness, and an acute understanding of the way the world really works. So long as you leverage other people's resources to create (intrinsic as well as perceived) value for large audiences, and consistently innovate, or leverage innovations from other fields into your own industry, you can accumulate a fortune of any magnitude.

Maxim #6. The Ultimate Sales Proposition is found by actually caring for the best interests of your customers, clients or readers.

This is the strategy that makes you pre-eminent. You actually think about their well-being and care about their well-being. You present to them opportunities that actually benefit them, and you will allow them to buy nothing less than the best possible experience they can buy.

You create a value proposition so well tailored to their needs that they cannot resist it. If they do resist it, it's simply because they don't understand it well enough just yet, and then it becomes your moral obligation to ensure that they understand it.

Maxim #7. Allocate your resources disproportionately.

The world arranges itself according to the 80/20 principle. That means that the top 20% of your products and services bring in almost 80% of your profits. That the top 20% of your clients bring in 80% of your profits. And that the top 20% of your activities produce 80% of your income.

20% of the assets in your portfolio produce 80% of the returns you get.

Eliminating or outsourcing the 80%, you can vastly improve the effectiveness of your time and other resources. Your marketing budget is best spent by focusing on the best prospects. Your follow up campaigns are best directed towards your most loyal clients.

The best assets you own deserve the lion's share of your investment capital.

If your resources are allocated disproportionately, in accordance with the natural law of 80/20, then you will accelerate your march towards financial freedom.

Maxim #8. Anything that brings in cashflow is an asset. Anything that takes out cashflow is a liability.

Prudent investors maximize their assets and minimize their liabilities. They keep their expenses to a minimum, and use the remainder of their total income to acquire assets.

Maxim #9. Allocate your income into separate bank accounts immediately.

Keep at least three bank accounts. One account for expenses, one for investments, and one for savings. As soon as you have some income, divide it into a pre-determined proportion, and distribute it into your accounts.

Maxim #10. Your primary goal as investor should be to achieve financial freedom through your investments.

You make investments so that they produce cashflow. Once you have made enough investments that the cashflow produced from the income takes care of all your expenses, and you still have something left over for reinvestment, then you are financially free. Financial freedom is the root of all freedom in life.

Maxim #11. Don't buy anything you don't need immediately or won't use regularly.

The bulk of your expenses should be predictable and fixed. Live a comfortable lifestyle, of course, but don't waste money on buying things that really have no utility in your life. Remember: Functional is beautiful.

FINAL NOTE

So there you have it. The keys to the kingdom. The rules of winning this game. The strategies for maximum impact.

Now go forth and conquer.

And remember...

<u>*The world works the way it works. Not the way you want it to.*</u>

www.ingramcontent.com/pod-product-compliance
Lightning Source LLC
Chambersburg PA
CBHW020905180526
45163CB00007B/2636